Wall Pilates Workouts Bible

[3 in 1]

The Ultimate 28-Day Challenge to Improve Flexibility, Strength and Balance | Wall Pilates Exercises for Women, Seniors, and Beginners

Clara Tillery

Table of Contents

INTRODUCTION

Welcome to the innovative and empowering world of Wall Pilates, a groundbreaking approach that harmonizes the fundamentals of Pilates with the steadfast support of a wall. In this enlightening journey, you'll uncover the remarkable benefits Wall Pilates has to offer, such as enhanced posture, increased flexibility, amplified muscle strength, effective injury prevention and rehabilitation, cardiovascular health, and myriad mental health benefits, including stress reduction, heightened mind-body connection, and improved sleep quality. This comprehensive guide will illuminate the core principles of Wall Pilates, unveiling its origins and distinctive tenets, including breath control, precision, core development, balance, and adaptability. You'll better understand how Wall Pilates diverges from traditional Pilates and contrasts with other low-impact exercise disciplines, such as yoga, tai chi, and barre.

We'll introduce you to the diverse equipment options available for Wall Pilates, demonstrating its inherent versatility and adaptability, making it a perfect fit for a wide array of individuals, including novices, seniors, pregnant and postpartum women, and athletes. Throughout this book, you'll acquire invaluable knowledge on essential techniques and principles, such as breathing techniques, alignment and posture, centering and core engagement, control and precision, fluidity and grace, and the indispensable mind-body connection. You'll also benefit from evidence-based insights on the efficacy of Wall Pilates and its profound impact on overall well-being.

In the final sections, we'll provide practical advice for embarking on your Wall Pilates journey, including crucial safety measures and guidance for initiating your practice. By the time you reach the end of this book, you'll possess the knowledge, tools, and motivation to harness the power of Wall Pilates, leading you towards a heightened level of fitness, strength, and well-being. So, let's embark on this transformative adventure together and unleash the potential of Wall Pilates!

PILATES FUNDAMENTALS

Getting bored during a Pilates class is almost impossible. That must be why this gymnastics on the mat is so popular with stars like Jennifer Aniston, Kaia Gerber and Bella Hadid. *What is pilates?* A discipline that allows for countless benefits that go even beyond toning. Doing Pilates requires absolute mastery of the body and lots of concentration. Invented by Joseph Hubertus Pilates, this gymnastics aims to create a balance between body, mind and spirit. As well as strengthening and shaping muscles to develop fluidity and precision in movements. Pilates, however, is not just a set of exercises, but a gymnastics with a philosophical and theoretical basis. The ultimate meaning of pilates is to merge body and mind, uniting - in a sense - Western physical disciplines with Eastern techniques.

At the core of Pilates is core control. It is the abdominals that allow one to maintain balance. And the control of the emotions allows stability to be achieved. A great workout in your 50s and a perfect sport for 40-year-olds, 30-year-olds, and even teenagers. Pilates is specifically built on six key principles: breathing, focus, center, control, precision, and fluidity. a field with many fascinating components that combine and interact.

If attention is necessary to get the muscles to move, breathing is essential to maintaining a strong mind-body connection.

On the other hand, maintaining control is the major goal of training. The ability to focus and move precisely can only be developed this way. In Pilates gymnastics, it is necessary to focus on the center to control the execution of movements and maintain fluidity. It is important to move with continuity.

All the Benefits of this Discipline

Over time, Pilates has gained popularity as a useful technique for enhancing physical health and wellbeing. With its unique combination of strengthening, stretching, and stabilizing movements, Pilates offers numerous benefits to practitioners of all ages and fitness levels. Let's delve into the many advantages of incorporating Pilates into your exercise routine, exploring its impact on physical health, mental well-being, and overall quality of life, supported by practical explanations based on scientific research.

Improved Posture

- **Strengthening postural muscles**: Pilates exercises target the deep muscles of the abdomen, back, and pelvic floor, collectively known as the "powerhouse" or "core." These muscles are crucial in maintaining proper posture (Emery, 2010). As a result, regular Pilates practice leads to a stronger and more stable core, providing the necessary support for optimal spinal alignment.

- **Alignment of the spine**: Pilates emphasizes the spine's natural curves and focuses on maintaining these curves during movement (Wells, 2014). This attention to spinal alignment helps correct imbalances and compensations that often lead to poor posture.

- **Reduction of muscle imbalances**: Pilates exercises address muscle imbalances by lengthening tight and weak muscles (Gallagher & Kryzanowska, 1999). This balanced approach promotes proper alignment and reduces the risk of postural problems.

- **Prevention and alleviation of back pain:** Pilates can effectively reduce chronic low back pain and improve functional movement (Wells, 2014; Rydeard et al., 2006). By targeting the core muscles and promoting proper spinal alignment, Pilates helps to alleviate and prevent back pain associated with poor posture.

Increased Flexibility

- **Enhanced range of motion:** Pilates exercises focus on lengthening and stretching the muscles while maintaining control and stability (Wells, 2014). This emphasis on flexibility helps to increase the range of motion in the joints, resulting in more fluid and efficient movement.

- **Reduced risk of injury:** Increased flexibility and range of motion can lead to a reduced risk of injury, as the body can better adapt and respond to physical stress (Emery, 2010). Pilates can help prevent injuries related to muscle imbalances, tightness, or lack of mobility by focusing on balanced muscle development and flexibility.

- **Improved muscular balance:** Pilates emphasizes the importance of balanced muscle development by targeting both the agonist and antagonist muscle groups (Gallagher & Kryzanowska, 1999). This approach ensures that muscles on both sides of a joint are equally strong and flexible, reducing the risk of injury and promoting overall muscular balance.

- **Alleviation of joint pain and stiffness:** Research suggests that Pilates can improve joint pain and stiffness, particularly in individuals with osteoarthritis (Cruz-Ferreira et al., 2011). Pilates can help alleviate joint pain and improve overall joint health by increasing flexibility and promoting balanced muscle development.

Enhanced Muscle Strength and Tone

- **Development of long, lean muscles:** Pilates exercises focus on eccentric muscle contractions, where the muscle lengthens while maintaining tension (Gallagher & Kryzanowska, 1999). This type of contraction is particularly effective at developing long, lean muscles without adding bulk.

- **Increased muscle endurance:** Pilates focuses on controlled, precise movements that require sustained muscle activation (Wells, 2014). As a result, regular Pilates practice can lead to increased muscle endurance, allowing you to perform daily activities and other exercises with greater ease and stamina.

- **Improved muscle balance and coordination:** Pilates exercises challenge the body's stabilizing muscles, which are crucial in maintaining balance and coordination (Emery, 2010). By targeting these muscles and promoting the development of a strong core, Pilates can help improve overall muscle balance and coordination.

- **Boosted metabolism and fat burning potential:** Pilates is not typically considered a high-intensity workout, but research suggests it can still contribute to increased calorie expenditure and fat burning potential (Di Lorenzo et al., 2018). Developing lean muscle mass through Pilates practice can also boost your resting metabolic rate, helping you burn more calories even when you're not exercising.

Injury Prevention and Rehabilitation

Strengthening of stabilizer muscles: Pilates exercises target the deep stabilizing muscles of the body, which are essential for maintaining proper alignment and preventing injury (Emery, 2010). Pilates can lessen the chance of damage during daily activities and other forms of exercise by strengthening these muscles, which can assist safeguard the joints.

Improvement of proprioception and balance: Pilates enhances body awareness and proprioception – the ability to sense your body's position in space (Gallagher & Kryzanowska, 1999). This heightened awareness can lead to improved balance and a reduced risk of falls, particularly in older adults (Bird et al., 2012).

Non-impact and low-impact exercise options: Pilates offers a variety of non-impact and low-impact exercise options, making it an ideal choice for individuals with joint pain, arthritis, or other conditions that may limit their ability to participate in high-impact activities (Cruz-Ferreira et al., 2011).

Rehabilitation from injuries and surgeries: Pilates is an effective tool for rehabilitation following injuries and surgeries, particularly for conditions affecting the musculoskeletal system (Keays et al., 2008). By focusing on controlled, precise movements and targeting the deep stabilizing muscles, Pilates can help facilitate a safe and efficient recovery process.

Cardiovascular Health

Improved circulation: Pilates exercises involve controlled breathing techniques, which can help increase blood oxygenation and circulation (Wells, 2014). Improved circulation can lead to better overall cardiovascular health and reduced risk of conditions such as hypertension.

Enhanced oxygen delivery to muscles: Combining deep breathing and targeted movement in Pilates can enhance oxygen delivery to the muscles, promoting more efficient energy production and reducing muscle fatigue (Wells, 2014).

Low-impact cardio workouts: While traditional Pilates exercises may not elevate the heart rate as much as high-intensity cardiovascular exercises, they can still improve cardiovascular fitness. Additionally, many Pilates classes and workouts now incorporate more dynamic movements and exercises designed to increase the heart rate and provide a low-impact cardio workout (Di Lorenzo et al., 2018).

Better heart health and reduced risk of heart disease: Regular participation in Pilates has been linked to improved heart health, including a reduced risk of heart disease and better management of conditions such as hypertension (Di Lorenzo et al., 2018). Pilates can play a valuable role in maintaining a healthy heart by promoting cardiovascular fitness.

Mental Health Benefits

Reduced Stress and Anxiety

- **Mindful movement and focused breathing:** Pilates emphasizes mindfulness and the connection between the body and breath, which can help reduce stress and anxiety by fostering a sense of calm and focus (Wells, 2014). This mind-body approach to exercise has been shown to reduce stress levels and improve overall mental health effectively (Brown & Ryan, 2003).

- **Release of endorphins:** Like other forms of exercise, Pilates can stimulate the release of endorphins – natural chemicals in the brain that help to alleviate pain and produce a sense of well-being (Gordon et al., 2008). Regular Pilates practice can improve mood and a more positive outlook on life.

- **Improvement of mood and emotional well-being:** Research has shown that regular participation in mind-body exercises like Pilates can lead to significant improvements in mood, emotional well-being, and overall mental health (Pilkington et al., 2005). Pilates can be valuable in fostering emotional resilience and well-being by reducing stress, anxiety, and negative emotions.

Increased Mind-Body Connection

- **Enhanced body awareness:** Pilates focuses on controlled, precise movements that require high body awareness and concentration (Gallagher & Kryzanowska, 1999). This emphasis on body awareness can help improve the mind-body connection, leading to a greater understanding of how the body moves and functions.

- **Development of mindfulness:** Pilates encourages mindfulness through focused breathing and movement, promoting a sense of presence and connection to the present moment (Wells, 2014). Regular mindfulness practice has been shown to have numerous mental health benefits, including reduced stress, anxiety, and depression (Brown & Ryan, 2003).

- **Improved concentration and focus:** The attention to detail and precision required in Pilates exercises can help improve concentration and focus (Gallagher & Kryzanowska, 1999). Pilates can improve cognitive function and overall brain health by cultivating a greater sense of mental clarity and focus.

Better Sleep

- **Relaxation and stress reduction:** The mind-body approach of Pilates, which emphasizes mindfulness, focused breathing, and controlled movement, can help promote relaxation and reduce stress levels (Wells, 2014). This relaxation response can contribute to better sleep quality by helping to calm the mind and prepare the body for rest.

- **Regulation of sleep-wake cycle:** Regular exercise, including Pilates, has been shown to improve the regulation of the sleep-wake cycle, leading to more consistent sleep patterns and better overall sleep quality (Youngstedt, 2005). Establishing a consistent exercise routine with Pilates can help support healthy sleep habits and improve overall sleep quality.

- **Improved sleep quality and duration:** Research has demonstrated that regular participation in mind-body exercises like Pilates can significantly improve sleep quality and duration (Pilkington et al., 2005). Pilates can contribute to more restorative and restful sleep by reducing stress and promoting relaxation.

Benefits For Special Populations

Pilates for Seniors

- **Safe and low-impact exercise**: Pilates offers a variety of non-impact and low-impact exercise options, making it an ideal choice for seniors who may be experiencing joint pain or other age-related physical limitations (Cruz-Ferreira et al., 2011).

- **Improved balance and fall prevention**: Pilates exercises target the deep stabilizing muscles and promote body awareness, contributing to improved balance and a reduced risk of falls in older adults (Bird et al., 2012).

- **Maintenance of bone density**: While Pilates is not a weight-bearing exercise like walking or running, it can still help to maintain bone density by promoting muscle strength and functional movement (Roller et al., 2009). Regular participation in Pilates can contribute to overall bone health and help to prevent age-related bone loss.

- **Enhanced functional movement and mobility**: Pilates focuses on functional movement patterns that mimic everyday activities, making it particularly beneficial for seniors who wish to maintain independence and mobility (Emery, 2010). By improving strength, flexibility, and balance, Pilates can help older adults continue to perform daily tasks with greater ease and confidence.

Pilates for Pregnant and Postpartum Women

- **Strengthening of the pelvic floor**: Pilates exercises often target the pelvic floor muscles, which can help maintain their strength and function during pregnancy and childbirth (Mazzarino et al., 2015). A strong pelvic floor can reduce the risk of pregnancy-related complications such as incontinence and pelvic organ prolapse.

- **Alleviation of back pain and discomfort**: The focus on core strength and spinal alignment in Pilates can help to alleviate pregnancy-related back pain and discomfort by providing greater support for the growing belly and reducing strain on the lower back (Mazzarino et al., 2015).

- **Improved posture and alignment**: As the body changes during pregnancy, maintaining proper posture and alignment becomes even more critical. By maintaining optimal alignment and strengthening the muscles that support the spine, Pilates workouts can help pregnant women maintain good posture. (Mazzarino et al., 2015).

- **Safe postpartum recovery and rehabilitation:** Pilates can be an effective tool for postpartum recovery, helping women to regain their strength, flexibility, and muscle tone after childbirth (Mazzarino et al., 2015). Pilates can facilitate a safe and efficient recovery process by focusing on the core and pelvic floor muscles while reducing the risk of complications such as diastasis recti and pelvic organ prolapse.

Pilates for Athletes

- **Cross-training and injury prevention:** Pilates can serve as an effective cross-training method for athletes, helping to balance out the demands of their primary sport by targeting often-neglected muscle groups and promoting overall muscle balance (Sáez-Sáez de Villarreal et al., 2013). This balanced approach to training can help prevent injuries and improve overall athletic performance.

- **Enhanced sports performance:** Pilates has been shown to improve core strength, balance, flexibility, and proprioception, all essential components of athletic performance (Sáez-Sáez de Villarreal et al., 2013). By incorporating Pilates into their training regimen, athletes can experience improvements in their sport-specific skills and overall performance.

- **Improved balance, flexibility, and strength:** The focus on core strength, flexibility, and balance in Pilates can help athletes improve these key aspects of their physical fitness, leading to better overall performance and a reduced risk of injury (Sáez-Sáez de Villarreal et al., 2013).

- **Faster recovery from intense workouts:** For faster recovery following strenuous workouts or contests, Pilates exercises can increase blood flow and oxygenation to the muscles (Wells, 2014). By incorporating Pilates into their training routine, athletes can enhance their recovery and reduce the risk of overtraining and injury.

Pilates vs. Other Gentle Exercise Disciplines

Pilates has long been recognized as an effective and safe form of exercise that can bring about a wide range of benefits to those who practice it regularly. In this paragraph, we will explore the unique aspects of Pilates and compare it with other gentle exercise disciplines, such as yoga, tai chi, and barre, highlighting the advantages of Pilates in terms of both physical and mental well-being.

Pilates vs. Yoga

- **Focus**: While Pilates and yoga emphasize the connection between the body and mind, Pilates focuses more on strengthening the core and improving muscle balance. Yoga, on the other hand, places greater emphasis on flexibility and spirituality.

- **Movements**: Pilates consists of controlled, precise movements, while yoga involves holding poses for an extended period. Pilates often requires specialized equipment, whereas yoga can be practiced on a mat with minimal props.

- **Breathing**: In Pilates, the breath is synchronized with movement to help engage the core and improve circulation. Yoga strongly emphasizes deep, diaphragmatic breathing to facilitate relaxation and meditation.

Pilates vs. Tai Chi

- **Origins**: Pilates comes from Western exercise, while tai chi is a martial art from China that has been around for hundreds of years and focuses on slow, flowing movements.

- **Movements**: Pilates' movements are typically more dynamic and challenging, targeting specific muscle groups for strength and flexibility. Tai chi, on the other hand, involves more fluid, circular movements designed to improve balance and coordination.

- **Energy Flow**: Tai chi strongly emphasizes the concept of "qi," or life energy, and seeks to harmonize this energy through mindful movements. Pilates does not incorporate this concept, focusing on the physical benefits of strengthening and stretching the body.

Pilates vs. Barre

Origins: While Pilates was developed as a holistic exercise system, barre is rooted in ballet and incorporates elements of Pilates, yoga, and strength training.

Movements: Pilates exercises often involve slow, controlled movements focusing on alignment and core strength. Barre utilizes small, isometric movements to target specific muscle groups, often incorporating light weights and resistance bands.

Equipment: Pilates often requires specialized equipment, such as the reformer or Cadillac, while barre typically uses a ballet barre, along with props like resistance bands and light weights.

Pilates Instrumentation

Before delving into the specific practice of Wall Pilates, it is essential to understand Pilates as a whole, including the various instruments and apparatuses utilized in traditional Pilates practice. This chapter will provide an in-depth look at the most common Pilates equipment, their purpose, and functionality, followed by a detailed exploration of Wall Pilates, the variant featured in this book.

Traditional Pilates Equipment

Reformer: this is one of the most well-known and widely used pieces of Pilates equipment. This versatile apparatus consists of a sliding carriage, springs for resistance, straps, and a footbar. The Reformer can be used for various exercises, targeting various muscle groups and allowing for a full-body workout. It helps improve strength, flexibility, balance, and coordination by providing resistance and support during exercise execution.

Cadillac (Trapeze Table): The Cadillac, also known as the Trapeze Table, is a large, stable apparatus resembling a four-poster bed. It features a variety of attachments, such as a trapeze bar, springs, straps, and a push-through bar. Many workouts on the Cadillac can work different body parts, such as the core, upper body, and lower body. It is particularly beneficial for rehabilitation, as it supports and assists in executing controlled movements.

Wunda Chair (Pilates Chair): The Wunda Chair, or Pilates Chair, is a compact piece of equipment that consists of a small, padded seat with a pedal and adjustable springs for resistance. The Wunda Chair can be used for various exercises that challenge balance, strength, and coordination, making it an excellent option for advanced Pilates practitioners and athletes.

Ladder Barrel: The Ladder Barrel is a curved, padded barrel attached to a ladder-like structure with adjustable rungs. It is primarily used for exercises that focus on spinal mobility, flexibility, and core strength. The Ladder Barrel allows for deep stretches and back extension exercises, promoting proper spinal alignment and overall posture.

Spine Corrector (Step Barrel): The Spine Corrector, also known as the Step Barrel, is a small, padded, curved apparatus designed to support the spine during various exercises. It is often used for exercises that target the core, hips, and shoulders and for deep stretching and spinal mobility movements.

Wall Pilates Equipment

Wall-Mounted Resistance Bands: Wall-mounted resistance bands are adjustable, elastic bands secured to the wall at various heights. They provide resistance during exercises, helping to improve strength, flexibility, and balance. Resistance bands can be used for a wide range of exercises, targeting different muscle groups and mimicking the resistance provided by the springs on traditional Pilates equipment.

Wall Straps: Wall straps are adjustable, secured to the wall, often used for assisted stretching and balance exercises. They can be utilized in various ways to support and enhance traditional Pilates movements, allowing for greater control and stability during the execution of the exercises (Anderson, 2009).

Wall Bars: Wall bars, also known as stall bars or Swedish bars, are a series of horizontal bars mounted on a vertical frame attached to the wall. They can be used for various exercises, including hanging, stretching, and strengthening movements. Wall bars offer various grip and support options for exercises challenging upper body strength, flexibility, and core stability (Anderson, 2009).

Wall-Mounted Ballet Barre: This horizontal bar is attached to the wall, typically used for ballet training and barre fitness classes. In Wall Pilates, the ballet barre can be utilized for balance and support during exercises focusing on lower body strength, flexibility, and coordination. It can also be used for stretching and core-strengthening exercises (Anderson, 2009).

Warning: If you don't have access to the specialized equipment mentioned above, don't worry! Performing Wall Pilates is also possible using free-body exercises that don't require any equipment. This bundle-book concludes with various free-body exercises developed for Wall Pilates practitioners of all levels. These exercises will allow you to enjoy Wall Pilates's benefits without investing in costly apparatuses. Stay tuned, and keep reading to discover how you can effectively practice Wall Pilates using your body weight and a suitable wall.

FOUNDATIONAL PRINCIPLES OF WALL PILATES

In the fitness world, it's common to see enthusiasts seeking new and innovative ways to spice up their exercise routines. Enter Wall Pilates, an unexpected yet surprisingly effective adaptation of the classic Pilates discipline that can leave even the most dedicated Pilates aficionado scratching their head. In this comprehensive chapter, we will dig into the interesting world of Wall Pilates, exploring its origins, benefits, and techniques, while highlighting this unconventional exercise approach's charm.

The Origins of Wall Pilates

While the precise origins of Wall Pilates may be elusive, there is no denying the resourcefulness and creativity of those who first embraced this unconventional approach to the classic Pilates discipline. Let's dive deeper into the story behind this innovative fitness trend.

It is said that the earliest practitioners of Wall Pilates were a small, dedicated group of fitness enthusiasts who came from diverse backgrounds, including dance, gymnastics, and physical therapy. Each member brought their unique perspectives and experiences to the table, resulting in a novel approach to Pilates that would eventually gain popularity in the fitness community.

As the story goes, these early adopters found themselves in a predicament when faced with a lack of space and equipment during a particularly busy Pilates session. Recognizing that they would have to think outside the box, they turned their gaze to the one surface they had yet to explore - the wall. By combining their collective knowledge of body mechanics, alignment, and movement, they experimented with the wall as a means of support, resistance, and balance.

Over time, these trailblazers refined their wall-based Pilates exercises, gradually expanding their repertoire and sharing their techniques with others in the fitness community. As more and more people began to discover the benefits of Wall Pilates, instructors and practitioners alike started to incorporate the wall into their routines, both as a way to challenge traditional Pilates exercises and to offer new options for individuals with limited mobility or strength.

Today, Wall Pilates has evolved into a widely recognized and respected form of exercise, with dedicated classes, workshops, and training programs available for those interested in learning more about this unique twist on traditional Pilates. The beauty of Wall Pilates lies not only in its adaptability and versatility but also in its testament to the power of human creativity and ingenuity in the face of limitations.

While the origins of Wall Pilates may be rooted in a moment of necessity, the practice has grown into a thriving discipline that continues to challenge and inspire millions of practitioners worldwide. In doing so, it serves as a reminder that the most unconventional ideas can sometimes lead to the most remarkable results.

The Principles of Wall Pilates

Wall Pilates may be unconventional in its approach, but it remains grounded in the foundational principles of traditional Pilates. Incorporating the wall as a central element in the practice adds a unique and dynamic dimension to these principles. Let's explore the core principles of Wall Pilates in greater detail.

Breath Control

As with traditional Pilates, breath control is critical in Wall Pilates. The practice encourages mindful, diaphragmatic breathing, which helps to engage the core muscles, improve circulation, and maintain focus during the exercises. The wall offers a unique opportunity to enhance breath control, as it provides a tactile reference point for deepening the awareness of one's breath and how it relates to movement.

Precision

Precision is a hallmark of Pilates, and Wall Pilates is no exception. The emphasis on precise, controlled movements is maintained throughout the practice, with the wall as a useful tool for maintaining proper alignment and form. By providing a stable surface against which to perform the exercises, the wall enables practitioners to focus on the quality and accuracy of their movements.

Core Development

Developing a strong, stable core is central to traditional and Wall Pilates. The abdominal, lower back, hip, and pelvic muscles — which support the spine and encourage effective movement patterns — are targeted by the exercises to be activated and strengthened. Wall Pilates takes this principle further by utilizing the wall as a source of resistance and support, offering additional challenges and opportunities for core engagement.

Balance

Balance is a crucial component of Pilates, and Wall Pilates places a particular emphasis on this principle. The wall offers a unique means of challenging and improving balance by providing a stable yet dynamic surface against which to perform exercises. By incorporating the wall into their practice, practitioners can develop a heightened sense of proprioception, or the awareness of one's body in space, contributing to overall balance and stability.

Adaptability

One of the key principles of Pilates is its adaptability to different fitness levels and individual needs. Wall Pilates upholds this principle by offering a range of exercises that can be modified or progressed to suit varying abilities and goals. The wall provides a versatile tool that can be used to make exercises more accessible for beginners or to add intensity and challenge for more advanced practitioners.

In summary, Wall Pilates stays true to the core principles of traditional Pilates while offering a unique and dynamic twist through the incorporation of the wall. By using the wall as a primary support, resistance, and balance tool, practitioners can experience a fresh perspective on Pilates that challenges and inspires.

Wall Pilates vs. Traditional Pilates

As the fitness world continues to evolve, innovative approaches to established disciplines emerge, offering new perspectives and challenges. Wall Pilates is one such adaptation of the traditional Pilates method, providing unique benefits and opportunities for growth. In this paragraph, we will delve into the distinct advantages of Wall Pilates compared to traditional Pilates, highlighting the key differences between the two variations and shedding light on the potential benefits of incorporating Wall Pilates into one's fitness routine.

Versatility and Adaptability

Traditional Pilates: Traditional Pilates offers various exercises that can be modified to suit different fitness levels and individual needs. However, some of the more advanced exercises may require specialized equipment, such as the reformer or Cadillac, which can be limiting for those without access to such apparatuses.

Wall Pilates: Wall Pilates enhances the adaptability of the practice by using the wall as a versatile tool that can be easily accessed in any setting. The wall allows for more modifications and progressions, making it an ideal option for individuals with limited mobility, strength, or space.

Balance and Proprioception

Traditional Pilates: Balance is crucial, with many exercises designed to challenge and improve stability. While traditional Pilates helps develop a strong sense of proprioception, the focus is primarily on core engagement and alignment.

Wall Pilates: Wall Pilates emphasizes balance by incorporating the wall into the exercises, providing a unique means of challenging and improving stability. The use of the wall promotes heightened proprioception, enhancing the awareness of one's body in space and contributing to overall balance and coordination.

Resistance and Intensity

Traditional Pilates: Resistance is often generated through specialized equipment or body weight. While this can provide an effective challenge, it may not offer the same resistance level as other fitness modalities, such as weight training or resistance bands.

Wall Pilates: The wall serves as a source of resistance in Wall Pilates, providing a dynamic and adjustable means of increasing the intensity of the exercises. By utilizing the wall for resistance, practitioners can easily modify the level of challenge to suit their individual needs and goals, allowing for a more personalized workout experience.

Accessibility and Convenience

Traditional Pilates: While traditional Pilates can be practiced on a mat without equipment, some exercises may be more effective or challenging when performed using specialized apparatuses. This can make traditional Pilates less accessible for those without access to a studio or the necessary equipment.

Wall Pilates: One of the main advantages of Wall Pilates is its accessibility and convenience. The wall is a readily available resource in most settings, making it easy for practitioners to incorporate Wall Pilates into their routines regardless of location or access to specialized equipment. This increased accessibility means that Wall Pilates can be practiced in various environments, such as at home, in the office, or even outdoors, providing a convenient and adaptable option for individuals with busy schedules or limited resources.

Body Awareness and Alignment

Traditional Pilates: A core principle is emphasizing body awareness and proper alignment. Practitioners are encouraged to focus on the precision and control of each movement, fostering a strong mind-body connection and promoting better posture and movement patterns.

Wall Pilates: Wall Pilates builds upon the principle of body awareness by using the wall as a tactile reference point for alignment and form. The wall provides immediate feedback on posture and positioning, enabling practitioners to make adjustments and corrections in real-time. This enhanced body awareness can lead to improved posture, reduced risk of injury, and greater overall movement efficiency.

Who is Wall Pilates ideal for?

As we have seen, Wall Pilates is an innovative adaptation of the traditional Pilates method and has gained popularity for its unique approach, versatility, and adaptability. *But who can benefit from Wall Pilates, and how does it cater to the diverse needs of different individuals?* The next few lines will answer exactly that!

Beginners

Example: Sarah is new to Pilates and feels intimidated by using specialized equipment or performing complex movements. She is looking for an accessible and beginner-friendly way to get started with Pilates.

How Wall Pilates Helps: Wall Pilates is an ideal option for beginners like Sarah, as it offers a range of exercises that can be easily modified to accommodate varying fitness levels and abilities. The wall provides support and stability, allowing Sarah to focus on developing proper form and alignment without feeling overwhelmed or discouraged.

Seniors

Example: John is a senior who wants to maintain strength, flexibility, and balance as he ages. He is concerned about the risk of falls and is looking for a safe and gentle exercise routine to help him stay active.

How Wall Pilates Helps: Wall Pilates is an excellent choice for seniors like John, as it emphasizes balance, stability, and functional movement, which are crucial for fall prevention and overall well-being. The wall offers additional support, allowing John to perform exercises and confidently minimize the risk of injury.

Individuals Recovering from Injuries

Example: Lisa is recovering from a knee injury and has been advised by her physical therapist to focus on low-impact exercises that strengthen her core and improve her overall muscle balance.

How Wall Pilates Helps: Wall Pilates can be a valuable tool in injury rehabilitation, as it offers a low-impact and adaptable approach to exercise. The wall provides support and resistance, enabling Lisa to perform exercises that target her core and stabilizing muscles without placing undue stress on her injured knee.

Pregnant and Postpartum Women

Example: Emily is in her second trimester of pregnancy and wants to maintain her fitness while preparing her body for childbirth. She is looking for a safe and effective exercise routine that can be adapted to her changing needs throughout pregnancy and beyond.

How Wall Pilates Helps: Wall Pilates is well-suited for pregnant and postpartum women like Emily, as it can be easily modified to accommodate the physical changes that occur during pregnancy and the postpartum period. The wall offers support and stability, allowing Emily to engage her core muscles and maintain proper alignment while reducing the risk of injury.

Athletes

Example: Mike is a competitive runner who wants to improve his balance, flexibility, and core strength to enhance his athletic performance. He is looking for a cross-training option that complements his existing training regimen.

How Wall Pilates Helps: Wall Pilates can serve as an effective cross-training tool for athletes like Mike, as it helps to develop balance, flexibility, and core strength, which are essential components of athletic performance. The wall provides a unique means of challenging and improving these skills, allowing Mike to target specific areas of weakness and enhance his running performance.

Embracing the Power of Wall Pilates

Throughout this comprehensive exploration of Wall Pilates, we have delved into its foundational principles, origins, and distinct advantages compared to traditional Pilates. We have also discussed how Wall Pilates caters to diverse individuals, including beginners, seniors, those recovering from injuries, pregnant and postpartum women, and athletes.

As we conclude this chapter, it is evident that Wall Pilates is not merely a novel adaptation of a well-established discipline but a transformative practice that opens new doors to growth, self-discovery, and physical well-being. By harnessing the wall's power as a versatile support, resistance, and balance tool, Wall Pilates transcends conventional boundaries and invites practitioners to challenge themselves in unique and inspiring ways. Whether you are new to Pilates or a seasoned practitioner seeking a fresh perspective, Wall Pilates offers an opportunity to embark on a journey of personal exploration and empowerment. As you embrace the principles of breath control, precision, core development, balance, and adaptability, you will cultivate a strong, flexible, and balanced body and discover the inner resilience and determination that lies within.

So, step up to the wall, and allow yourself to be guided by the wisdom and innovation of Wall Pilates. Embrace the challenges, celebrate the victories, and immerse yourself in a practice that can transform your physical fitness, mindset, and life. The journey begins with a single breath and a commitment to push past limitations to pursue your true potential. Welcome to the world of Wall Pilates – *a world of endless possibilities, growth, and self-discovery.*

MASTERING THE ESSENTIAL TECHNIQUES AND PRINCIPLES

As we embark on the exciting journey of Wall Pilates, we invite you to explore and embody its foundational principles, which serve as the building blocks for a practice that is as much about self-discovery as physical fitness. In this chapter, we will delve into the essential elements that define the unique and dynamic practice of Wall Pilates, uncovering the magic that unfolds when we merge mindful movement with the powerful support of the wall. From breathing techniques that anchor us in the present moment to the cultivation of fluidity and grace in our movements, we will illuminate the path towards a harmonious balance between the mind and body. Together, we will explore the following foundational principles:

- Breathing Techniques: Discover the profound impact of breath on our physical and mental well-being, as we learn to harness the power of deep, intentional breathing in our Wall Pilates practice.

- Alignment and Posture: Unveil the importance of proper alignment and posture as the basis for efficient movement and injury prevention, and learn how the wall can serve as a tactile guide for achieving optimal alignment.

- Centering and Core Engagement: Delve into the vital role of centering and core engagement in our Wall Pilates practice, as we awaken the powerhouse within and establish a stable foundation from which to move and flow.

- Control and Precision: Embrace the challenge of performing each movement with control and precision, as we develop greater body awareness, coordination, and mastery over our physical form.

- Fluidity and Grace: Explore the art of moving with fluidity and grace, as we learn to integrate the principles of Wall Pilates into seamless, flowing sequences that nourish the body, mind, and spirit.

- Mind-Body Connection: Unravel the deep connection between our thoughts, emotions, and physical movements, as we cultivate mindfulness and presence in our Wall Pilates practice, empowering ourselves to reach new heights of self-discovery and personal growth.

As you immerse yourself in the rich tapestry of Wall Pilates, allow yourself to be guided by these foundational principles, embracing the opportunity to connect with your innermost self and unlock your limitless potential. This journey is one of growth, transformation, and empowerment, as we learn to harness the power of the wall and our inner strength to create a inspiring and life-affirming practice. Welcome to the world of Wall Pilates, where the possibilities for growth and self-discovery are boundless, and the path to mastery begins with a single, mindful breath.

Breathing Techniques

Breathing is essential to any Pilates practice, and Wall Pilates is no exception. It fuels our bodies with oxygen and connects our minds with our movements. In this chapter, we will explore the importance of breath in Wall Pilates, as well as practical and research-based techniques to help you harness the power of your breath and elevate your practice to new heights. Let's look at all the benefits involved:

- Enhances Oxygen Delivery: Effective breathing techniques improve the amount of oxygen delivered to the muscles and organs, encouraging optimal performance and improving all aspects of physical functioning.

- Promotes Mind-Body Connection: Focusing on the breath helps to cultivate mindfulness, allowing for a deeper connection between the mind and body and fostering greater body awareness.

- Facilitates Core Engagement: Coordinated breathing aids in engaging the core muscles, providing a stable foundation for controlled and precise movements.

- Reduces Stress and Tension: Deep, intentional breathing has a calming effect on the nervous system, helping to release tension and stress while promoting relaxation and mental clarity.

Diaphragmatic Breathing (Abdominal Breathing)

How to Practice: Make sure your spine is in neutral alignment while you stand with your back to the wall. Put your hands on your abdomen and inhale slowly and deeply through your nose, letting your tummy expand. Exhale slowly through your lips, pulling your navel toward your spine as you do so. Focus on maintaining a steady rhythm, and aim for 4-6 breaths per minute.

Benefits: Diaphragmatic breathing encourages full lung expansion, increasing oxygen delivery to the muscles and organs. It also promotes relaxation and helps to activate the core muscles.

Lateral Breathing (Ribcage Breathing)

How to Practice: Stand facing the wall with your back against it and your spine in a neutral position. Place your hands on the sides of your ribcage, with your fingertips touching. Inhale deeply through your nose, expanding your ribcage to the sides while keeping your abdomen relatively still. Exhale through your mouth, feeling your ribcage contract and your fingertips moving closer together. Aim for a steady rhythm of 6-8 breaths per minute.

Benefits: Lateral breathing enhances lung capacity and oxygen delivery while allowing for greater core engagement and stabilization during Wall Pilates exercises.

Coordinated Breathing

How to Practice: Coordinate your breath with each movement as you perform Wall Pilates exercises. Generally, inhale during a movement's preparation or initiation phase, and exhale as you execute the movement. For example, when performing a wall squat, inhale as you lower yourself into the squat, and exhale as you push back up to the starting position.

Benefits: Coordinated breathing helps to maintain a strong mind-body connection, enhance core engagement, and improve overall movement quality and efficiency.

Research-Based Insights on Breathing in Pilates

A. The Effects of Pilates Breathing on Respiratory Function: Research has shown that practicing Pilates breathing techniques can improve lung function, muscle strength, and overall respiratory efficiency (*Hagins M, States R, Selfe T, Innes K. (2013)*.

B. The Role of Breathing in Core Activation: Studies have found that coordinating breath with movement during Pilates exercises can result in greater activation of the core muscles, leading to improved stability and movement control *(Emery K, De Serres SJ, McMillan A, Côté JN. (2010)*.

Alignment and Posture

Alignment and posture are fundamental components of Wall Pilates, as they serve as the foundation for efficient movement and play a crucial role in injury prevention. In this chapter, we will explore the importance of proper alignment and posture in Wall Pilates, as well as practical and research-based techniques to help you achieve optimal form and maximize the benefits of your practice. Let's look at all the benefits involved:

- Enhances Movement Efficiency: Proper alignment and posture facilitate efficient movement patterns, ensuring that the body works optimally and that energy is not wasted on compensatory movements.

- Reduces Injury Risk: Maintaining correct alignment and posture minimizes stress on the joints, muscles, and ligaments, reducing the risk of injury during Wall Pilates exercises.

- Promotes Core Engagement: Optimal alignment and posture require the engagement of the core muscles, which provides a stable foundation for controlled and precise movements.

- Improves Body Awareness: Focusing on alignment and posture increases awareness and proprioception, helping you better understand your body and its movement capabilities.

Establishing Neutral Spine

How to Practice: Stand with your back to the wall and your feet hip distance apart. Maintain a small space between your lower back and the wall by engaging your core muscles. Ensure your head, shoulders, and hips align, and your chin is parallel to the floor. This is your neutral spine position.

Benefits: Maintaining a neutral spine during Wall Pilates exercises helps to protect the spine and promote proper core engagement.

Shoulder and Head Alignment

How to Practice: Stand in neutral spine against the wall. Draw your shoulder blades down and back, allowing them to rest naturally against the wall. Ensure that the back of your head is also gently touching the wall. Keep your neck long, relaxed, and your chin parallel to the floor.

Benefits: Proper shoulder and head alignment helps to prevent neck and shoulder tension, promote efficient movement, and reduce the risk of injury.

Pelvic Alignment

How to Practice: Stand in neutral spine against the wall, with your feet hip-width apart. Focus on maintaining a level pelvis by engaging your core muscles and avoiding excessive hips tilting. Imagine a bowl of water resting on your pelvis; your goal is to keep the water from spilling.

Benefits: Maintaining optimal pelvic alignment supports spine health, improves balance, and enhances overall movement efficiency.

Research-Based Insights on Alignment and Posture in Pilates

A. The Role of Pilates in Improving Posture: Studies have shown that practicing Pilates can lead to significant improvements in posture, particularly in individuals with postural imbalances or musculoskeletal pain *(La Touche R, Escalante K, Linares MT. (2018).*

B. The Effects of Pilates on Spinal Alignment: Research suggests that regular Pilates practice can help improve spinal alignment, contributing to a reduction in pain and discomfort associated with spinal misalignments *(Wells C, Kolt GS, Bialocerkowski A. (2012).*

Centering and Core Engagement

Centering and core engagement are essential elements of Wall Pilates, as they provide a stable foundation for controlled, precise, and efficient movement. In this chapter, we will explore the importance of centering and core engagement in Wall Pilates, as well as practical and research-based techniques to help you connect with your center and maximize the benefits of your practice. Let's look at all the benefits involved:

- Enhances Movement Efficiency: Proper core engagement and centering allow for more efficient movement patterns, ensuring that the body works optimally and energy is not wasted on compensatory movements.

- Improves Balance and Stability: A strong, engaged core provides stability and balance during Wall Pilates exercises, reducing the risk of injury and promoting optimal performance.

- Facilitates Proper Alignment: Engaging the core muscles supports the spine and helps maintain proper alignment and posture throughout Wall Pilates movements.

- Fosters Mind-Body Connection: Focusing on centering and core engagement enhances body awareness and deepens the connection between the mind and body, leading to a more mindful and effective practice.

Finding Your Center

How to Practice: Stand with your back against the wall in a neutral spine position. Place your hands on your lower abdomen and imagine a point approximately two inches below your navel and two inches inward. This is your center, also known as the "powerhouse" in Pilates. Focus on connecting with this point throughout your Wall Pilates practice.

Benefits: Connecting with your center helps to anchor your movements and provides a focal point for core engagement and energy distribution.

Engaging the Core Muscles

How to Practice: Draw your navel slightly inward toward your spine while keeping your spine and pelvis in neutral positions against the wall. This activates your deep core muscles, including the transversus abdominis. Maintain this gentle engagement throughout your Wall Pilates exercises.

Benefits: Engaging the core muscles provides stability, supports proper alignment, and enhances movement efficiency during Wall Pilates practice.

Core Strengthening Exercises

- **Wall Plank:** Stand facing the wall with your hands at shoulder height, slightly wider than shoulder-width apart. Step back into a plank position, engaging your core and maintaining a straight line from your head to your heels. Hold for 30-60 seconds, focusing on deep, steady breaths.

- **Wall Leg Lifts**: Standing with your back to the wall and your feet hip distance apart. Maintaining touch with the wall, engage your core as you slowly elevate one leg straight before you. Hold for 5 to 10 seconds, then let go and do the opposite.

- **Wall Squats:** Stand with your back to the wall and your feet slightly in front of your hips. Keep your back against the wall as you steadily lower into a squat stance while engaging your core. Hold for 10 to 30 seconds before standing back up.

Research-Based Insights on Centering and Core Engagement in Pilates

A. The Role of Pilates in Core Strength and Stability: Studies have shown that practicing Pilates can lead to significant improvements in core strength, stability, and endurance, resulting in better performance in daily activities and reduced risk of injury *(Sekendiz B, Altun Ö, Korkusuz F, Akın S. (2017)*.

B. The Effects of Pilates on Postural Control and Balance: Research suggests that regular Pilates practice can help improve postural control and balance, particularly in older adults and individuals with balance impairments *(Nolan M, Nordon-Craft A, Egan B, Kehl K, Stevens Lobo V, Kleidon T, Cogan D, Neufer PD. (2018).*

Control and Precision

Control and precision are integral components of Wall Pilates, as they contribute to developing efficient, safe, and effective movement patterns. In this chapter, we will explore the importance of control and precision in Wall Pilates, as well as practical and research-based techniques to help you refine your movements and maximize the benefits of your practice. Let's look at all the benefits involved:

- Enhances Movement Efficiency: Focusing on control and precision ensures that the body works optimally, minimizing wasted energy and promoting efficient movement patterns.

- Reduces Injury Risk: Controlled, precise movements reduce the risk of injury by minimizing unnecessary strain on the joints, muscles, and ligaments.

- Develops Body Awareness: Concentrating on control and precision enhances body awareness and proprioception, allowing for greater understanding and mastery of your body and its movement capabilities.

- Facilitates Mind-Body Connection: Focusing on control and precision deepens the connection between the mind and body, leading to a more mindful and effective practice.

Moving with Intention

How to Practice: Approach each Wall Pilates exercise with a clear intention, focusing on the specific muscles involved and the desired movement pattern. This mental focus will help you maintain control and precision throughout your practice.

Benefits: Moving with intention promotes efficiency, reduces the risk of injury, and fosters a deeper mind-body connection.

Slowing Down Your Movements

How to Practice: Perform each Wall Pilates exercise at a slow, controlled pace, allowing yourself ample time to engage the appropriate muscles and maintain proper alignment fully. Gradually increase the tempo while maintaining control and precision as you become more proficient.

Benefits: Slower, controlled movements help develop body awareness, enhance movement efficiency, and reduce the risk of injury.

Emphasizing Quality Over Quantity

How to Practice: Focus on performing each Wall Pilates exercise with the highest control and precision possible, even if it means doing fewer repetitions. Prioritizing quality over quantity will lead to greater mastery of the movements and a more effective practice.

Benefits: Emphasizing quality over quantity helps develop proper movement patterns, enhances body awareness, and promotes long-term progress.

Research-Based Insights on Control and Precision in Pilates

A. The Role of Pilates in Motor Control and Neuromuscular Efficiency: Studies have shown that practicing Pilates can lead to significant improvements in motor control and neuromuscular efficiency, resulting in better movement patterns and reduced risk of injury (*Emery K, De Serres SJ, McMillan A, Côté JN. (2010)*.

B. The Effects of Pilates on Proprioception and Body Awareness: Research suggests that regular Pilates practice can help improve proprioception and body awareness, essential for maintaining control and precision during movement *(Curnow D, Cobbin D, Wyndham J, Boris Choy ST. (2009)*.

Fluidity and Grace

Fluidity and grace are essential aspects of Wall Pilates that contribute to developing smooth, harmonious, and aesthetically pleasing movement patterns. This chapter will explore the importance of fluidity and grace in Wall Pilates and practical and research-based techniques to help you cultivate these qualities in your practice. Let's look at all the benefits involved:

- Enhances Movement Efficiency: Fluid, graceful movements promote efficient energy transfer and minimize energy waste, leading to an overall more effective practice.

- Reduces Injury Risk: Smooth, coordinated movements reduce the risk of injury by minimizing stress on the joints, muscles, and ligaments.

- Develops Body Awareness: Focusing on fluidity and grace enhances awareness and proprioception, allowing for greater understanding and mastery of your body's movement capabilities.

- Fosters Mind-Body Connection: Concentrating on fluidity and grace deepens the connection between the mind and body, leading to a more mindful and enjoyable practice.

Breathing and Movement Coordination

How to Practice: Coordinate your breath with your movements in Wall Pilates exercises, using the inhale to prepare and the exhale to execute each movement. This breath-movement coordination helps create a natural rhythm and flow in your practice.

Benefits: Coordinating breath and movement promotes fluidity, enhances body awareness, and fosters a deeper mind-body connection.

Smooth Transitions

How to Practice: Focus on seamless transitions between Wall Pilates exercises, maintaining control and engagement throughout the sequence. This attention to smooth transitions helps create a continuous flow in your practice.

Benefits: Smooth transitions promote fluidity, enhance movement efficiency, and reduce the risk of injury.

Developing Core Stability

How to Practice: Engage your core muscles throughout your Wall Pilates practice to provide a stable foundation for fluid, graceful movements. A strong, stable core allows smoother, more controlled movements and transitions.

Benefits: Core stability promotes fluidity, reduces the risk of injury, and enhances movement efficiency.

Research-Based Insights on Fluidity and Grace in Pilates

The Role of Pilates in Coordination and Movement Quality: Studies have shown that practicing Pilates can lead to significant improvements in coordination, movement quality, and overall body awareness, resulting in more fluid and graceful movement patterns. *(Bernardo LM. (2007).*

The Effects of Pilates on Flexibility and Range of Motion: Research suggests that regular Pilates practice can help improve flexibility and range of motion, essential for achieving fluidity and grace in movement. *(Latey P. (2001).*

Mind and Body Connection

The mind-body connection is a crucial aspect of Wall Pilates that sets it apart from other forms of exercise. This chapter will delve into the importance of the mind-body connection in Wall Pilates and practical and research-based techniques to help you cultivate this essential connection in your practice.

- Enhances Movement Efficiency: A strong mind-body connection allows greater movement control, leading to more efficient and effective movement patterns.

- Reduces Injury Risk: Being in tune with your body enables you to identify potential issues and adjust to prevent injuries.

- Develops Body Awareness: Cultivating the mind-body connection enhances awareness and proprioception, allowing a greater understanding of your body's movement capabilities.

- Fosters Emotional Well-being: A stronger sense of well-being and general mental wellness can result from connecting with your body more profoundly.

Focused Breathing

How to Practice: Incorporate focused breathing techniques into your Wall Pilates practice. Concentrate on the rhythm and depth of your breath, and coordinate your breath with your movements. This mindful approach to breathing helps to deepen the mind-body connection.

Benefits: Focused breathing promotes relaxation, reduces stress, and enhances body awareness.

Mindful Movement

How to Practice: Approach each Wall Pilates exercise with intention and full awareness. Be present in the moment and pay attention to the sensations in your body as you move. This mindfulness will help you develop a stronger connection with your body.

Benefits: Mindful movement enhances body awareness, promotes relaxation, and fosters a deeper connection between the mind and body.

Visualization

How to Practice: Use visualization techniques to imagine your body moving smoothly and effortlessly through each Wall Pilates exercise. This mental rehearsal can help reinforce the mind-body connection and improve physical performance.

Benefits: Visualization enhances body awareness, boosts confidence, and fosters a deeper mind-body connection.

Research-Based Insights on the Mind-Body Connection in Pilates

A. The Role of Pilates in Enhancing Mindfulness: Studies have shown that practicing Pilates can lead to significant improvements in mindfulness and overall well-being, suggesting a strong connection between Pilates practice and the development of a deeper mind-body connection *(Caldwell K, Adams M, Quin R, Harrison M, Greeson J. (2013).*

B. The Effects of Pilates on Stress Reduction and Emotional Health: Research suggests that regular Pilates practice can help reduce stress, anxiety, and depression, demonstrating the importance of the mind-body connection in promoting overall emotional health. *(Cruz-Ferreira A, Fernandes J, Laranjo L, Bernardo LM, Silva A. (2011).*

Bottom line

Throughout this chapter, we have delved into the essential techniques and principles that form the foundation of a successful and fulfilling Wall Pilates practice. By understanding and implementing these vital components—breathing techniques, alignment and posture, centering and core engagement, control and precision, fluidity and grace, and the mind-body connection—you will be well-equipped to embark on a transformative journey towards optimal health and well-being.

As you continue to explore and refine your Wall Pilates practice, remember that consistency, patience, and dedication are key to unlocking the full potential of this unique and powerful discipline. Be open to learning, adapting, and growing with your practice, and embrace Wall Pilates's numerous physical, mental, and emotional benefits.

It is important to remember that Wall Pilates is more than just a series of exercises—it is a holistic approach to health and well-being emphasizing the interconnectedness of the mind, body, and spirit. By cultivating the essential techniques and principles outlined in this chapter, you will transform your Wall Pilates practice and foster a deeper self-awareness, resilience, and balance in all aspects of your life.

PREPARING FOR PRACTICE

Imagine standing at the edge of a vast, uncharted landscape, with the promise of discovery, growth, and transformation. This is the exciting world of Wall Pilates, a unique and dynamic discipline that will challenge and inspire you in ways you never thought possible. As you embark on this thrilling adventure, gathering the knowledge, tools, and resources needed to navigate this new terrain with confidence, safety, and ease is essential.

In this chapter we will be your trusty guide, illuminating the path and providing valuable insights as you embark on your Wall Pilates journey. We'll delve into the essential aspects of Wall Pilates that every intrepid explorer should know before setting out, along with practical tips and strategies for starting your practice on the right foot—or, in this case, the right wall.

From the fundamentals of Wall Pilates to the safety measures that will protect you as you push your boundaries and expand your horizons, we'll ensure you are well-equipped for the challenges and rewards.

Whether you're an experienced Pilates practitioner seeking new heights or a curious adventurer stepping into the world of Wall Pilates for the first time, this chapter will be your compass, pointing you in the right direction as you embark on a journey of self-discovery, empowerment, and holistic well-being. So, strap on your metaphorical hiking boots and prepare to conquer the vertical frontier of Wall Pilates, where untold treasures of strength, flexibility, and inner harmony await.

Things to Know Before Starting Wall Pilates

As you embark on your Wall Pilates journey, you must familiarize yourself with the unique aspects and best practices that will light your path towards a safe, enjoyable, and effective practice. This chapter will delve into the crucial aspects and practical advice that every aspiring Wall Pilates practitioner should know before venturing into this exciting discipline. Consider this your trusty compass, guiding you towards a successful and fulfilling practice.

- **Wall Selection and Preparation:** Choose a sturdy, smooth, and free of obstructions, such as wall hangings or shelves. You'll be relying on the wall for support and balance, so ensuring it can handle your weight and movements is essential. Clean the wall's surface to remove dust or dirt that might cause you to slip during your practice.

- **Using the Wall for Support and Resistance:** Learn how to use the wall as a tool for support, resistance, and balance. For example, pressing your hands or feet against the wall can create resistance during various exercises, while leaning against the wall can support balance and alignment. Mastering these techniques is essential to maximize the benefits of your Wall Pilates practice.

- **Adjusting Exercise Intensity:** Understand how to adjust the intensity of Wall Pilates exercises by modifying your distance from the wall or altering the angle of your body.

This allows you to tailor your practice to your fitness level and individual needs while maintaining proper alignment and form.

- **Wear Comfortable and Appropriate Clothing:** Opt for comfortable, breathable, and form-fitting clothing that allows unrestricted movement. Avoid baggy clothes or items with zippers, buttons, or embellishments that could interfere with your practice or cause discomfort against the wall.

- **Incorporating Wall Pilates-Specific Props:** Explore using specialized props such as wall straps, Pilates rings, and resistance bands, which can enhance and diversify your Wall Pilates practice. These tools can help you target specific muscle groups, increase resistance, and improve stability during your workout.

- **Warm-Up and Stretch:** Always begin your practice with a proper warm-up and stretching routine to prepare your muscles and joints for the exercises ahead. This not only enhances your performance but also reduces the risk of injury.

- **Developing Proper Alignment with the Wall:** Learn how to use the wall to improve your alignment and body awareness during practice. The wall can be a reference point to ensure your spine, pelvis, and shoulders are correctly aligned and engaged during various exercises.

- **Progress Gradually:** It's crucial to progress at a pace appropriate for your fitness level and experience. Start with basic exercises and gradually build upon them as you become more comfortable and proficient. Avoid pushing yourself too hard too soon, which can lead to injury or burnout.

By understanding and implementing these Wall Pilates-specific aspects and best practices, you'll be well-prepared to embark on your journey towards a safe, enjoyable, and effective practice. Use this knowledge as your compass, guiding you towards a successful and fulfilling Wall Pilates experience.

Tips for Starting the Practice

Here are some less common, yet highly effective tips from my years of experience teaching Wall Pilates that can help you improve your practice, accelerate progress, and enhance your overall physical fitness and inner well-being:

- **Use the "Powerhouse":** Wall Pilates, like traditional Pilates, focuses on the "Powerhouse" muscles, which include your deep abdominals, lower back, pelvic floor, and glutes. Always initiate movements from these muscles to improve your practice, creating a stable foundation and engaging your core throughout each exercise.

- **Focus on alignment and posture:** Proper alignment and posture are crucial for effective Wall Pilates practice. During each exercise, be mindful of your body's alignment, especially your spine. Avoid arching your lower back by keeping your neck aligned with your spine.

- **Use your breath effectively:** In Wall Pilates, breath control is essential. Coordinate your breath with each movement, inhaling during the preparation phase and exhaling during the exertion phase. This will help you engage your core, maintain proper alignment, and improve overall body awareness.

- **Progress gradually:** Increase the complexity of exercises as you gain strength, flexibility, and confidence in your practice to expedite growth and prevent injuries. Start with basic exercises and, over time, introduce more advanced movements or variations.

- **Develop body awareness:** Wall Pilates is an excellent opportunity to develop body awareness. Pay close attention to your body's sensations, learning to identify tension, discomfort, or imbalance areas. You can make necessary adjustments and enhance your overall practice by tuning into your body.

- **Be consistent and patient:** Consistency is key to improving your Wall Pilates practice and overall physical fitness. Aim to practice at least 2-3 times weekly, allowing adequate rest between sessions. Remember that progress takes time, so be patient and trust the process.

- **Integrate mindfulness and meditation**: Incorporate mindfulness and meditation into your Wall Pilates practice to enhance your inner well-being. Focus on the present moment, allowing thoughts to come and go without judgment. This can help reduce stress, improve mental clarity, and promote a greater sense of overall balance.

- **Seek feedback and guidance**: If possible, work with an experienced Wall Pilates instructor who can provide personalized feedback and guidance to help you refine your technique and deepen your practice. Alternatively, consider recording your practice sessions to review and identify areas for improvement.

- **Customize your practice**: Every individual is unique, and your Wall Pilates practice should reflect your specific needs, goals, and limitations. Modify exercises as needed and be willing to experiment with different movements or variations to find what works best for you.

- **Celebrate progress and achievements**: Acknowledge and celebrate your progress and achievements, no matter how small. By recognizing your accomplishments and enjoying the journey, you'll be more motivated to continue your Wall Pilates practice and reap the long-term benefits of improved physical fitness and inner well-being.

Warnings and Safety Measures in Wall Pilates

Wall Pilates, like any exercise, carries inherent risks if not performed properly or if certain precautions are overlooked. This chapter aims to provide an extensive and highly accurate overview of the warnings and safety measures you should know while practicing Wall Pilates. Adhering to these simple rules may reduce your chance of injury and ensure a risk-free and productive workout.

- **Consult a healthcare professional**: Before starting a Wall Pilates program, consult with your healthcare provider, especially if you have pre-existing medical conditions, injuries, or are pregnant. They can offer personalized guidance on appropriate modifications or restrictions to ensure your safety during practice.

- **Warm-up and cool-down:** Always include a proper warm-up before starting your Wall Pilates session to prevent injuries and prepare your body for the workout. Incorporate dynamic stretches and gentle movements that target the major muscle groups. Similarly, allocate time for a cool-down at the end of your session, focusing on static stretches and relaxation techniques.

- **Maintain proper alignment and form:** One of the most critical safety measures in Wall Pilates is maintaining proper alignment and form throughout each exercise. Incorrect alignment can place unnecessary stress on your joints, muscles, and spine, increasing the risk of injury. Pay close attention to your body's positioning, especially your neck, spine, and pelvis, and make adjustments as needed.

- **Progress at your own pace:** It's essential to progress at a pace appropriate for your fitness level and physical abilities. Avoid pushing yourself too hard, too quickly, as this can lead to injuries or exacerbate existing conditions. Gradually increase the difficulty of your exercises as you build strength, flexibility, and confidence.

- **Use appropriate modifications:** If you have limitations or are recovering from an injury, utilize modifications to ensure you perform each exercise safely and effectively. Consult with a qualified Wall Pilates instructor for personalized guidance on appropriate modifications based on your needs.

- **Choose a suitable practice space:** Select a clear space of any obstacles, providing ample room to move freely. Ensure your wall is sturdy and free of protrusions or sharp edges. Use a non-slip mat or soft surface for your feet to prevent slipping and provide adequate support.

- **Listen to your body:** Pay close attention to how your body feels during your Wall Pilates practice. If you experience pain, discomfort, or fatigue, stop the exercise immediately and assess the cause. Remember that it's always better to err on caution and avoid pushing your body beyond its limits.

- **Stay hydrated:** Proper hydration is essential for a safe and effective Wall Pilates practice. Drink water before, during, and after your session to maintain optimal hydration levels and support your body's recovery process.

- **Seek professional guidance**: If you're new to Wall Pilates or unsure about your technique, consider working with a qualified instructor who can provide personalized feedback and guidance. They can help you learn proper form, alignment, and exercise progressions, ensuring a safe and effective practice.

By adhering to these warnings and safety measures, you can significantly reduce the risk of injury and enhance the overall effectiveness of your Wall Pilates practice. Always prioritize safety, listen to your body, and consult a healthcare professional or qualified instructor to ensure a positive and beneficial workout experience.

CONCLUSION

Congratulations on completing the first volume of this bundle-book! You are now equipped with the essential knowledge and tools to embark on your Wall Pilates journey. As you begin to incorporate Wall Pilates into your fitness routine, remember that the true beauty of this practice lies in its adaptability and transformative power. As you embark on this new path, stay open to growth and embrace the process of self-discovery. Take the time to reflect on your short-term and long-term goals, and be prepared to adjust them as you progress. It's essential to recognize that every individual's journey is unique, and your practice should reflect your specific needs, desires, and aspirations.

Remember the importance of consistency, patience, and self-compassion as you work towards improving your physical fitness and inner well-being. Acknowledge and celebrate your achievements, no matter how small they may seem, and remember that every step forward is a testament to your dedication and resilience. In the words of Joseph Pilates, the creator of the Pilates method, *"Change happens through movement, and movement heals."* So, as you step into the world of Wall Pilates, embrace the movement and allow it to become an integral part of your life, healing and transforming you from the inside out.

May your Wall Pilates practice catalyze positive change and personal growth, inspiring you to reach new heights in your fitness journey and beyond. Here's to a healthier, stronger, and more balanced version of you!

BOOK 2: WALL PILATES FOR BEGINNERS

INTRODUCTION

Welcome to the practical part of Wall Pilates, designed to meet the specific needs of beginners, seniors, and women. This comprehensive exercise book will guide you through routines and exercises designed to support your fitness journey, regardless of age, experience, or physical condition.

To ensure a safe and effective workout, we will begin with the essential warm-up and cool-down exercises, emphasizing their importance in preventing injury and promoting recovery. You'll learn simple warm-up and cool-down routines that you can easily incorporate into your regular practice and purpose-focused exercises. These routines are 5 minutes long and 7 minutes long, respectively. Next, we will present a series of exercises suitable for beginners, focusing on the upper, middle and lower body. Each exercise is carefully selected and explained to ensure a solid foundation and a gradual increase in strength, flexibility and balance.

As you progress through the book, you will encounter specific exercises designed to address key aspects of your fitness journey, such as balance, flexibility, posture, and coordination. These exercises will hone your Wall Pilates skills and help you achieve your fitness goals more effectively.

This Wall Pilates exercise book is the perfect companion for embracing a healthier, stronger, and more balanced lifestyle. With my expert guidance and easy-to-follow instructions, you will be well on your way to unleashing the transformative power of Wall Pilates, specially designed for beginners, seniors and women. Let's begin this exciting journey together and discover the incredible benefits Wall Pilates has in store for you!

WARM-UP AND COOL-DOWN

The practice of Wall Pilates offers a wide array of physical and mental benefits, contributing to increased flexibility, strength, and overall well-being. However, the key to reaping these rewards is following a well-rounded routine with two essential components: warm-up and cool-down. Both stages are crucial in preparing the body for the upcoming workout and promoting a safe, injury-free training experience. In this chapter, we will delve into the foundations of warm-up and cool-down in Wall Pilates, highlighting their importance in the practice and emphasizing their role in maintaining proper form and safety.

The Importance of Warm-Up

The warm-up phase is an integral part of any Wall Pilates routine. It serves as the foundation upon which an effective and safe workout is built. During this stage, practitioners engage in gentle movements and stretches, gradually increasing the heart rate and blood flow to the muscles. The primary objectives of a warm-up are:

- **Increased Blood Flow:** Elevating the heart rate enhances blood circulation, ensuring muscles receive adequate oxygen and nutrients. This increased blood flow prepares the muscles for more strenuous activities, reducing the risk of injury. Additionally, improved circulation helps remove waste products, such as lactic acid, from the muscles, contributing to better overall performance and endurance.

- **Enhanced Muscle Flexibility and Joint Mobility:** Gentle stretching and dynamic movements during warm-up improve muscle elasticity and joint range of motion. This prepares the body for more challenging Wall Pilates exercises, preventing strains and sprains. Properly warmed-up muscles and joints are more responsive and less prone to injury, allowing practitioners to execute movements with greater precision and control.

- **Improved Neuromuscular Activation:** Warming up helps to activate the neuromuscular system, increasing the communication between the brain and the muscles. This results in better muscle recruitment and motor coordination, crucial for executing complex Wall Pilates movements with proper form and technique.

- **Temperature Regulation:** A good warm-up routine raises the body's core temperature, vital for optimal muscle function. Warmer muscles are more pliable and less prone to injury, making them better equipped to handle the challenges of a Wall Pilates session.

- **Mental Preparation:** A well-designed warm-up routine helps establish a mind-body connection, allowing practitioners to mentally prepare for the Wall Pilates workout ahead. This heightened focus enables better technique and body awareness, essential for effective training. Additionally, the warm-up phase sets the tone for the entire workout, cultivating a positive mindset and promoting motivation and discipline.

In light of these benefits, it becomes evident that a thorough warm-up is crucial for maximizing the effectiveness of a Wall Pilates session. By incorporating a combination of cardiovascular exercises, dynamic stretches, and activation movements, practitioners can ensure they are fully prepared – both physically and mentally – for the challenges that lie ahead in their Wall Pilates practice.

The Importance of Cool Down

The cool-down phase is the other vital aspect of any Wall Pilates routine, serving as the bridge between an intense workout and a return to a state of rest. This stage involves engaging in gentle movements, stretches, and relaxation techniques, allowing the body to recover and transition safely from the workout. The primary objectives of a cool-down are:

- **Restoration of Normal Heart Rate and Blood Pressure:** One can gradually restore normal heart and blood pressure rates by performing a cool-down regimen. This prevents dizziness and fainting, which may occur if the body is not given time to adjust after an intense workout. A gradual cool-down also helps to maintain venous return, ensuring that blood continues to flow back to the heart, preventing blood pooling in the extremities.

- **Reduction of Muscle Soreness and Stiffness:** Gentle stretches and relaxation exercises during the cool-down phase aid in releasing tension and reducing muscle soreness. This fosters faster recovery and allows practitioners to maintain a consistent training schedule. Stretching during the cool-down phase can also improve flexibility and mobility, enhancing overall performance in Wall Pilates exercises.

- **Improved Lactic Acid Removal:** A cool-down helps to remove lactic acid and other waste products generated during the workout. By engaging in low-intensity movements and stretches, practitioners can promote better circulation, facilitating the removal of these waste products, which can contribute to muscle soreness and fatigue if not adequately addressed.

- **Mental Relaxation and Reflection:** The cool-down period also serves as a time for mental relaxation and reflection. It encourages practitioners to focus on their breath, allowing them to release stress and tension, while acknowledging the efforts they put into their Wall Pilates session. This practice of mindfulness and gratitude can contribute to a more positive and fulfilling exercise experience, promoting mental well-being alongside physical fitness.

- **Injury Prevention and Maintenance of Physical Progress:** A consistent cool-down routine after each Wall Pilates session can aid in injury prevention and ensure the maintenance of the progress achieved in flexibility, strength, and overall fitness. By allowing the body to recover and reset, practitioners can avoid overtraining and minimize the risk of injuries that could hamper their progress and overall health.

In conclusion, a well-executed cool-down is as essential as a warm-up in Wall Pilates practice. Practitioners can ensure optimal recovery, injury prevention, and overall well-being by understanding this phase's importance and incorporating gentle movements, stretches, and relaxation techniques. Incorporating a cool-down routine into every Wall Pilates session allows individuals to reap the full benefits of their training, while promoting a sustainable and enjoyable fitness journey.

Warm-Up Exercises

Upper body

Neck rotations:

1. Put your feet hip-width apart and stand tall.

2. Bring your chin toward your chest gradually.

3. Make a circle with your head by rotating it to the right, tilting it back, and turning it to the left.

4. Repeat 5 times in each direction.

Shoulder rolls:

1. Put your feet hip-width apart and stand tall.

2. Slowly roll your shoulders forward in a circular motion 5 times.

3. Repeat, rolling shoulders backward 5 times.

Arm circles

1. Stand tall with your arms to the sides and your feet hip-width apart.

2. Rotate your arms in a series of progressively larger circles.

3. Continue for 30 seconds, then reverse the direction for another 30 seconds.

Wrist circles

1. Put your arms out in front of you, palms down.

2. Slowly rotate your wrists clockwise 10 times.

3. Rotate your wrists counterclockwise 10 times.

Core:

Cat-Cow stretch

1. Begin on your hands and knees, placing your wrists under your shoulders and your knees under your hips.

2. Take a deep breath, arch your back, and lift your chest and tailbone upward (Cow pose).

3. Pull your chin and tailbone in as you exhale and round your spine (Cat pose).

4. Repeat for 5-8 breath cycles.

Bird Dog

1. From a kneeling position, place your wrists under your shoulders and your knees under your hips.

2. Keep your left leg back and right arm extended, parallel to the ground.

1. Keep holding for 5 seconds before going back to the starting position.

2. Repeat with the right leg and left arm.

3. Keep alternating sides for 10 reps on each side.

Standing side bends

1. Stand tall with your hands on your hips and your feet hip-width apart.

2. Keep your hips steady while slowly bending your torso to the right.

3. Bend to the left and then back to the center.

4. On each side, repeat for 10 times.

Hip circles

1. Hands should be on hips while you stand with your feet hip-width apart.

2. Rotate your hips 10 times in a clockwise circular manner.

3. Repeat, rotating hips counterclockwise for 10 reps.

Lower body:

Leg swings:

1. Stand next to a wall for support and balance.

2. Swing your right leg forward and backward in a controlled motion.

3. Perform 10 swings, then switch to the left leg.

Ankle circles

1. Stand next to a wall for support and balance.

2. Rotate your ankle 10 times clockwise while lifting your right foot off the ground.

3. Repeat counterclockwise, then switch to the left foot.

Knee raises:

1. Stand tall with your feet hip-width apart.

2. While maintaining a straight back, lift your right knee toward your chest.

3. Repeat with the left knee, returning your right foot to the floor.

4. Continue alternating for 10 reps on each side.

Hamstring curls:

1. Stand tall with your feet hip-width apart.

2. Lift your right foot toward your glutes while bending your right knee.

3. Repeat with your left leg, returning your right foot to the floor.

4. Keep alternating for 10 reps on each side.

Cool-Down Exercises

Upper body

Neck stretch

1. Sit or stand tall with your shoulders relaxed.

2. With a slight rightward head tilt, tuck your ear close to your shoulder.

3. Hold for 15 to 20 seconds before switching sides.

Shoulder stretch

1. Put your feet hip-width apart and stand tall.

2. With your left hand, gently pull the elbow on your right arm as you extend it over your chest.

3. Hold for 15 to 20 seconds before switching sides.

Triceps stretch

1. Put your feet hip-width apart and stand tall.

2. Raise your right arm above you, bending the elbow so your hand can touch your lower back.

3. Pull your right elbow gently with your left hand.

4. Hold for 15 to 20 seconds before switching sides.

Chest stretch

1. Put your feet hip-width apart and stand tall.

2. Straighten your arms and join your fingers behind your back.

3. Open your chest and raise your hands toward the ceiling.

4. Hold for 15-20 seconds.

Core

Seated forward fold

1. Stretch your legs in front of you as you sit on the ground.

2. Inhale, and as you exhale, reach for your toes while keeping your back straight.

3. Maintain the position for 15 to 20 seconds.

Seated twist

1. Sit with your legs extended on the floor.

2. Place your right foot outside your left thigh by bending your right knee.

3. Put your left elbow on your right knee while rotating your torso to the right.

4. Keep still for 15 to 20 seconds before switching sides.

Child's pose

1. Kneel on the ground with your big toes touching and your knees hip-width apart.

2. Place your forehead on the ground while leaning back on your heels and reaching your arms forward.

3. Keep still for 30 seconds.

Lower body

Butterfly stretch

1. Knees should be pointed outward while you sit on the ground with your feet together at the soles.

2. Holding your feet, slowly lower your knees to the floor.

3. Keep still for 15-20 seconds.

Seated hamstring stretch

1. Place your left foot against your right thigh while sitting on the floor with your right leg outstretched.

2. Reach for your right foot while keeping your back straight.

3. Keep still for 15 to 20 seconds before switching sides.

Quadriceps stretch

1. Stand tall, holding onto a wall for support if needed.

2. Grab your right foot with your right hand while bending your right knee.

3. Pull your foot toward your glutes gently.

4. Keep still for 15 to 20 seconds before switching sides.

Calf stretch

1. Put your hands on the wall as you stand facing it for support.

2. Step back with your right foot, heel planted and toes pointed forward.

3. Lean into the wall until you feel a stretch in your right calf.

4. Keep still for 15 to 20 seconds before switching sides.

Hip flexor stretch

1. Kneel on your right knee, putting your left foot forward, forming a 90-degree angle with your left knee.

2. Gently push your hips forward, feeling a stretch in your right hip flex

3. Hold for 15 to 20 seconds before switching sides.

The Perfect 5-Minute Warm-Up Routine

As we have seen, warming up before a workout is an essential step often overlooked by many. A well-rounded warm-up routine prepares your body for the physical activity ahead, increasing blood flow, improving joint mobility, and reducing the risk of injury. Below, we present the Perfect 5-Minute Warm-Up Routine, designed to engage all major muscle groups and set you up for success in your workout. In just 5 minutes, this easy-to-follow warm-up routine will help you:

● Gradually increase your heart rate and circulation.

● Loosen up your joints and muscles.

- Enhance your flexibility and mobility.

- Mentally prepare for your workout, allowing you to focus and perform at your best.

Stay tuned as we walk you through each exercise, step-by-step, and get ready to elevate your workout experience!

Neck rotations (Upper body):

- Repetitions: 5 circles per direction

- Sets: 1

- Reason: To gently stretch and warm up the neck muscles and increase mobility.

Shoulder rolls (Upper body):

- Repetitions: 5 rolls per direction

- Sets: 1

- Reason: To loosen the shoulder joints and warm the muscles around the shoulders and upper back.

Arm circles (Upper body):

- Repetitions: 10 circles per direction

- Sets: 1

- Reason: Increase blood flow to the arms, warm the shoulder muscles, and improve shoulder mobility.

Cat-Cow stretch (Core):

- Repetitions: 5-8 breath cycles

- Sets: 1

- Reason: To warm up the spine, engage the core muscles, and improve spinal flexibility.

Bird Dog (Core):

- Repetitions: 5 reps per side

- Sets: 1

- Reason: To engage and warm up the core and lower back muscles while improving balance and stability.

Hip circles (Lower body):

- Repetitions: 10 circles per direction

- Sets: 1

- Reason: To loosen up the hip joints and warm up the muscles around the hips and pelvis.

Ankle circles (Lower body):

- Repetitions: 10 circles per direction

- Sets: 1

- Reason: To warm up the ankle joints and improve ankle mobility.

Knee raises (Lower body):

- Repetitions: 5 reps per side

- Sets: 1

- Reason: To warm up the hip flexors and improve hip mobility.

The Ultimate 7-Minute Cool-Down Routine

After an intense workout, allowing your body to cool down, stretch, and recover is crucial. The Ultimate 7-Minute Cool-Down Routine is specifically designed to help you ease into a state of relaxation while promoting muscle recovery and flexibility. This comprehensive cool-down routine targets all major muscle groups and helps alleviate post-workout soreness, preparing your body for your next fitness challenge. By dedicating just 7 minutes to this cool-down routine, you will:

- Gradually lower your heart rate and transition your body from a high-energy state to a state of rest.

- Enhance muscle recovery and reduce the risk of injury.

- Improve flexibility and joint mobility for better overall performance.

- Experience mental relaxation and a sense of accomplishment after your workout.

Get ready to unwind and recharge with our step-by-step guide to the Ultimate 7-Minute Cool-Down Routine, your essential companion to an effective workout!

Neck stretch (Upper body):

- Repetitions: 1 per side

- Sets: 1

- Hold: 15-20 seconds

- Reason: To gently stretch the neck muscles and improve flexibility.

Shoulder stretch (Upper body):

- Repetitions: 1 per side

- Sets: 1

- Hold: 15-20 seconds

- Reason: To stretch the shoulder muscles and release tension.

Triceps stretch (Upper body):

- Repetitions: 1 per side

- Sets: 1

- Hold: 15-20 seconds

- Reason: To stretch the triceps and promote relaxation.

Chest stretch (Upper body):

- Repetitions: 1

- Sets: 1

- Hold: 15-20 seconds

- Reason: To stretch the chest muscles and improve posture.

Seated forward fold (Core):

- Repetitions: 1

- Sets: 1

- Hold: 15-20 seconds

- Reason: To stretch the lower back and hamstrings.

Seated twist (Core):

- Repetitions: 1 per side

- Sets: 1

- Hold: 15-20 seconds

- Reason: To stretch the spine and core muscles.

Child's pose (Core):

- Repetitions: 1

- Sets: 1

- Hold: 30 seconds

- Reason: To release tension in the back, shoulders, and hips.

Butterfly stretch (Lower body):

- Repetitions: 1

- Sets: 1

- Hold: 15-20 seconds

- Reason: To stretch the inner thighs and hip muscles.

Seated hamstring stretch (Lower body):

- Repetitions: 1 per side

- Sets: 1

- Hold: 15-20 seconds

- Reason: To stretch the hamstrings and promote flexibility.

Quadriceps stretch (Lower body):

- Repetitions: 1 per side

- Sets: 1

- Hold: 15-20 seconds

- Reason: To stretch the quadriceps and improve flexibility.

Calf stretch (Lower body):

- Repetitions: 1 per side

- Sets: 1

- Hold: 15-20 seconds

- Reason: To stretch the calf muscles and alleviate tension.

Throughout this chapter, we have explored the critical importance of warm-up and cool-down routines, ensuring that your body is well-prepared for a workout and adequately recovers afterward. Incorporating these essential practices into your fitness regimen lays the groundwork for a successful and transformative fitness journey.

As we transition into the next chapter, "Wall Pilates Exercises for Beginners," you are now equipped with a comprehensive understanding of the warm-up and cool-down exercises that will complement and enhance your Pilates practice. The knowledge you've gained in this chapter will improve your performance, reduce the risk of injury, and aid in muscle recovery.

Remember that your fitness journey is a marathon, not a sprint. Dedication, consistency, and proper body care are vital to achieving your goals and maintaining a healthy, balanced lifestyle. By embracing the power of warm-up and cool-down routines, you are taking a significant step towards unlocking your full potential and reaping the rewards of a well-rounded fitness routine.

EXERCISES FOR BEGINNERS

Upper Body

Wall Push-ups

Step-by-step directions:

1. Standing with your back to the wall and your shoulders wide apart, place your palms flat against the wall at shoulder height.

2. Maintaining a straight line from your head to your heels while inhaling and engaging your core.

3. Take a breath, flex your elbows, and drop your chest toward the wall.

4. To return to the beginning position, inhale and push away from the wall.

Easier alternative: Move your feet closer to the wall to decrease the angle and make the push-ups less challenging.

Expert advice: To activate your triceps and safeguard your shoulders, keep your elbows close to your torso.

Progression: Increase the distance between your feet and the wall to make the exercise more challenging.

Target muscles: Chest, shoulders, and triceps

Purpose: Upper body strength and muscle toning

Wall Angels

Step-by-step directions:

1. Hang your legs at your sides, your feet hip-width apart, and your knees slightly bent.

2. Press your lower back, shoulders, and head against the wall.

3. With your elbows bent 90 degrees and the backs of your hands touching the wall, extend your arms to the sides at shoulder height.

4. Inhale and slide your arms up the wall, straightening them as much as possible without losing contact with the wall.

5. As you exhale, bring your arms back to where they were before.

Easier alternative: Perform the exercise with your arms extended and palms facing the wall, maintaining contact between your wrists and the wall.

Expert advice: Keep your ribcage down and core engaged to prevent arching your lower back.

Progression: Hold light dumbbells or a resistance band in your hands while performing the exercise.

Target muscles: Shoulders, upper back, and chest

Purpose: Shoulder mobility, posture, and upper body flexibility

Wall Tricep Dips

Step-by-step directions:

1. Stand a few inches away from the wall with your back to the wall and your feet hip-width apart.

2. Place your palms flat on the wall behind you, slightly lower than shoulder height, and fingers pointing down.

3. Lower your body toward the ground by engaging your core and bending your elbows.

4. To raise your body back to the beginning position, extend your arms straight.

Easier alternative: Bend your knees and position your feet closer to the wall to reduce the intensity.

Expert advice: Keep your elbows close to your body to engage your triceps and protect your shoulders.

Progression: Increase the distance between your feet and the wall or perform the exercise on an unstable surface, like a BOSU ball, for added difficulty.

Target muscles: Triceps and shoulders

Purpose: Upper body strength and muscle toning

Wall Press Up

Step-by-step directions:

1. Place your palms shoulder-width apart and flat against the wall while standing facing the wall.

2. Engage your core and lean into the wall, bending your elbows to the sides.

3. To return to the beginning position, push away from the wall while straightening your arms.

Easier alternative: Position your feet closer to the wall to decrease the angle and make the exercise less challenging.

Expert advice: Maintain a straight line from your head to your heels throughout the exercise.

Progression: Perform the exercise on an unstable surface, like a BOSU ball, for added difficulty.

Target muscles: Chest, shoulders, and triceps

Purpose: Upper body strength, muscle toning, and balance

Wall Bicep Curl

Step-by-step directions:

1. Standing in front of the wall, place your palms shoulder-width apart, flat against the wall, and point your fingers down toward the floor.

2. Keep your feet firmly planted as you engage your core and lean back.

3. Pull your chest toward the wall while bending your elbows.

4. To return to the beginning position, extend your arms straight.

5. Do 10–15 reps.

Easier alternative: Position your feet closer to the wall to decrease the angle and make the exercise less challenging.

Expert advice: Maintain a straight line from your head to your heels throughout the exercise.

Progression: Perform the exercise with one arm at a time for added difficulty.

Target muscles: Biceps and forearms

Purpose: Upper body strength, muscle toning, and endurance

Wall Rows

Step-by-step directions:

1. With your back to the wall and your arms shoulder-width apart, place your hands flat against the wall.

2. Keep your feet firmly planted as you engage your core and lean back.

3. Squeezing your shoulder blades together, lift your chest against the wall while bending your elbows.

4. To return your body to the beginning position, straighten your arms.

5. Do 10–15 reps.

Easier alternative: Position your feet closer to the wall to decrease the angle and make the exercise less challenging.

Expert advice: Maintain a straight line from your head to your heels throughout the exercise.

Progression: Perform the exercise on an unstable surface, like a BOSU ball, for added difficulty.

Target muscles: Upper back, shoulders, and biceps

Purpose: Upper body strength, posture, and muscle balance

Wall Lateral Raises

Target muscles: Shoulders and upper back

Purpose: Shoulder strength, stability, and muscle definition

Step-by-step directions:

1. Standing with your feet hip-width apart and your right side against the wall.

2. Put your right palm flat and at shoulder height on the wall.

3. Keeping your left arm straight and engaging your core, steadily lift it until it is parallel to the floor.

4. Return your left arm to your side.

5. After 10 to 15 reps, switch sides.

Easier alternative: Perform the exercise with a smaller range of motion, raising your arm only as high as comfortably possible.

Expert advice: Maintain a tall posture and avoid leaning on the wall during the exercise.

Progression: Hold a light dumbbell or resistance band in the working arm to increase the difficulty.

Wall Shoulder Press

Target muscles: Deltoids, triceps, and upper back muscles

Purpose: Strength and stability

Step-by-step directions:

1. Place your palms flat against the wall at shoulder height and slightly wider than shoulder-width apart while facing the wall.

2. Engage your core and lean into the wall, bending your elbows to the sides and lowering your forehead toward the wall.

3. Push away from the wall while straightening your arms to return to where you started.

4. Repeat for 10-15 times.

Easier alternative: Position your feet closer to the wall to decrease the angle and make the exercise less challenging.

Expert advice: Maintain a straight line from your head to your heels throughout the exercise.

Progression: Perform the exercise on an unstable surface, like a BOSU ball, for added difficulty.

Wall Plank with Alternating Shoulder Taps

Target muscles: Core, shoulders, and chest

Purpose: Strength and balance

Step-by-step directions:

1. Standing with your back to the wall and your hands slightly wider than shoulder-width apart, flat against the wall at shoulder height.

2. Step back into a plank position with your body straight from your head to your heels by contracting your abdominal muscles.

3. Your right hand should tap your left shoulder before you put it back on the wall.

4. Next, back your hand on the wall and tap your right shoulder with your left one.

5. For each side, repeat for 10 to 15 times.

Easier alternative: To decrease the angle, exercise with your feet closer to the wall.

Expert advice: Maintain a stable core and avoid rotating your hips during the shoulder taps.

Progression: Increase the speed of the shoulder taps for added difficulty.

Wall Assisted Reverse Fly

Target muscles: Upper back, rear deltoids, and rhomboids

Purpose: Strength and posture

Step-by-step directions:

1. Stand with your back to the wall, your arms out in front of you, and your hands flat against the wall at shoulder height.

2. Engage your core and lean your body slightly toward the wall.

3. Keeping your arms straight, slide your hands out to the sides, bringing your shoulder blades closer together.

4. Return to the initial position by sliding your hands back together.

5. Repeat for 10–15 repetitions.

Easier alternative: Perform the exercise with a smaller range of motion, moving your hands only as far apart as comfortably possible.

Expert advice: Keep your neck relaxed and maintain a neutral spine throughout the exercise.

Progression: Hold light dumbbells or a resistance band in your hands to increase the difficulty.

Core

Wall Roll Down

Step-by-step directions:

1. Place your feet hip-width apart and slightly away from the wall as you stand with your back to the wall.

2. Draw your navel toward your spine as you inhale to activate your core.

3. By forcing your back against the wall while exhaling, rolling down one vertebra at a time, and tucking your chin toward your chest.

4. As far as you can descend without having to lift your feet off the ground. At the bottom, inhale.

5. As you carefully roll back up to a standing posture, exhale and stack each vertebra against the wall.

Easier alternative: Bend your knees slightly while rolling down to make the movement easier.

Expert advice: Throughout the exercise, make sure your head, shoulders, and lower back remain in contact with the wall by maintaining an even weight distribution on your feet.

Target muscles: Hamstrings, lower back, and abdominal muscles

Purpose: Flexibility, spine mobility, and posture

Wall Plank

Step-by-step directions:

1. Place your palms against the wall shoulder height and width apart while facing the wall.

2. Maintain a straight line from your head to your heels by engaging your core and moving your feet back until you are in a plank position.

3. Keeping your breath even, maintain the plank for 30 to 60 seconds.

Easier alternative: Hold the plank for 10 to 15 seconds, then gradually lengthen the hold as your strength improves.

Expert advice: Keep your neck and spine neutral, and avoid dropping your hips or lifting your buttocks during the plank.

Target muscles: Abdominals, shoulders, and lower back

Purpose: Core strength, shoulder stability, and balance

Wall Supported Dead Bug

Step-by-step directions:

1. Legs should be at a 90-degree angle and flat on the wall while you lay on the floor.

2. Arms might be at your sides or resting on your stomach.

3. Put your back against the floor while engaging your core.

4. Slowly extend your right leg, keeping your heel on the floor and gliding it down the wall.

5. Repeat with the left leg while returning to the beginning position.

Easier alternative: Slide your heel only partway down the wall, keeping the movement within a comfortable range of motion.

Expert advice: Keep your lower back firmly pressed to the floor during the exercise.

Target muscles: Abdominals, hip flexors, and lower back

Purpose: Core strength, balance, and coordination

Wall Assisted Bicycle Crunch

Target muscles: Obliques, rectus abdominis, and hip flexors

Purpose: Core strength and stability

Step-by-step directions:

1. Legs should be hip-width apart, flat against the wall, and your knees should be 90 degrees bent.

2. Lift your head, neck, and shoulders off the ground by placing your hands behind your head.

3. Slide your right heel up the wall while you engage your core and bring your right elbow to your left knee.

4. Bringing your left elbow nearer your right knee, repeat on the other side before returning to the beginning position.

5. Keep alternating sides for 10-15 repetitions on each side.

Easier alternative: Don't lift your head, neck, or shoulders off the floor while exercising.

Expert advice: Maintain a neutral spine and avoid pulling on your neck during the exercise.

Progression: Perform the exercise without the wall, lifting and twisting your legs in the air.

Wall Mountain Climbers

Target muscles: Core, shoulders, and hip flexors

Purpose: Core strength and cardiovascular endurance

Step-by-step directions:

1. Place your palms flat against the wall at shoulder height and slightly wider than shoulder-width apart while facing the wall.

2. Step back into a plank position with your body straight from your head to your heels by contracting your abdominal muscles.

3. Return to the starting position after bringing your right knee toward your chest while keeping your foot off the ground.

4. Repeat the movement with your left knee.

5. Continue alternating legs for 10–15 repetitions on each side.

Easier alternative: Perform the exercise at a slower pace, or decrease the range of motion by bringing your knees only partway toward your chest.

Expert advice: Throughout the exercise, maintain a straight line from your head to your heels and refrain from bouncing your hips.

Progression: Increase the speed of the mountain climbers for added cardiovascular challenge or perform the exercise on an unstable surface, like a BOSU ball, for increased difficulty.

Wall Bridge

Target muscles: Core, glutes, and hamstrings

Purpose: Strength and stability

Step-by-step directions:

1. Legs should be hip-width apart, flat against the wall, and your knees should be 90 degrees bent.

2. Pressing your feet against the wall, engage your core and raise your hips.

3. After two to three seconds in the bridge posture, return your hips to the floor.

4. Repeat for 10–15 times.

Easier alternative: Perform the bridge exercise without the wall, keeping your feet flat on the floor.

Expert advice: Keep your core engaged and avoid overarching your lower back during the exercise.

Wall Scissor Kicks

Target muscles: Core and hip flexors

Purpose: Core strength and stability

Step-by-step directions:

1. With your legs outstretched and your heels resting against the wall, lie on your back.

2. Put your back into the floor and engage your core.

3. Lift your right leg off the wall and lower it toward the floor, while keeping your left leg extended and resting against the wall.

4. Change legs, bringing your left leg closer to the floor and bringing your right leg back to the wall.

5. Repeat for 10–15 repetitions on each side.

Easier alternative: Your feet should be flat on the wall as you exercise with your knees bent.

Expert advice: Keep your lower back in contact with the floor throughout the exercise.

Wall Russian Twists

Target muscles: Obliques and core

Purpose: Core strength and stability

Step-by-step directions:

1. Kneel on the floor with your back to the wall, feet flat on the ground, and your knees bent.

2. Engage your core and lean back slightly, pressing your lower back into the wall.

3. Clasp your hands in front of you or place them on your chest.

4. After turning your torso to the right and touching your right elbow to the wall, do the same thing on your left side.

5. Keep alternating sides for 10-15 repetitions on each side.

Easier alternative: Perform the exercise without the wall, keeping your back off the wall and rotating only as far as comfortably possible.

Expert advice: Keep your core engaged and maintain a neutral spine throughout the exercise.

Wall Supported Leg Circles

Target muscles: Core, hip flexors, and inner and outer thighs

Purpose: Core strength and flexibility

Step-by-step directions:

1. With your legs outstretched and your heels resting against the wall, lie on your back.

2. Put your back into the floor and engage your core.

3. While maintaining your left leg extended and resting against the wall, lift your right leg off the ground and make a tiny circle in the air.

4. Repeat for 10-15 repetitions, then switch to the left leg.

Easier alternative: Your feet should be flat on the wall as you exercise with your knees bent.

Expert advice: Keep your lower back in contact with the floor throughout the exercise.

Wall Plank with Knee Tucks

Target muscles: Core, hip flexors, and shoulders

Purpose: Core strength and balance

Step-by-step directions:

1. Place your palms flat against the wall at shoulder height and slightly wider than shoulder-width apart while facing the wall.

2. Step back into a plank position with your body straight from your head to your heels by contracting your abdominal muscles.

3. Return to the beginning position by bringing your right knee toward your chest while keeping your foot off the ground.

4. Use your left knee to repeat the movement.

5. Continue alternating legs for 10-15 repetitions on each side.

Easier alternative: Perform the exercise slower or decrease the range of motion by bringing your knees only partway toward your chest.

Expert advice: Throughout the exercise, maintain a straight line from your head to your heels and refrain from bouncing your hips.

Lower Body

Wall Pelvic Curl

Step-by-step directions:

1. Put your feet hip-width apart and your knees bent at a 90-degree angle as you lay on the floor on your back.

2. Lie down on the floor with your arms by your sides.

3. Inhale and engage your core.

4. With each exhalation, you can raise your spine one vertebra at a time by placing your feet on the wall and slowly raising your hips off the floor.

5. Take a deep breath at the top, then let it out as you slowly roll your spine back to the ground.

Easier alternative: Do not lift your hips as high, rolling up only to the comfortable point.

Expert advice: Keep your knees aligned with your hips and ankles throughout the exercise.

Target muscles: Hamstrings, glutes, and lower back

Purpose: Pelvic stability, lower body strength, and spine mobility

Wall Supported Clamshells

Step-by-step directions:

1. Stand with your feet hip-width apart, facing the wall, and approximately an arm's length away.

2. Lean forward and rest your arms at shoulder level against the wall.

3. Step your feet back slightly and bend your knees, engaging your core.

4. Lift your right knee out to the side while keeping your feet together. Do not shift your pelvis.

1. Lower your right knee, then do the same on the left side.

Easier alternative: Perform the exercise lying on your side, with your legs bent and heels together.

Expert advice: Keep your pelvis stable and avoid leaning on the wall during the exercise.

Target muscles: Glutes, hip abductors, and hip external rotators

Purpose: Hip stability, lower body strength, and muscle toning

Wall Supported Scissor Kicks

Step-by-step directions:

1. Your heels should be against the wall as you lay on the floor on your back with your legs extended.

2. Place your hands underneath your lower back for support, or rest them by your sides.

3. Look at your legs while you engage your core and lift your head, neck, and shoulders off the floor.

4. Inhale and lower your right leg, sliding your heel down the wall.

5. As you exhale, lift your right leg, slip your heel back up the wall, and lower your left leg simultaneously.

6. Continue alternating legs for 10-15 repetitions.

Easier alternative: Throughout the exercise, maintain a flat back, neck, and shoulders.

Expert advice: Maintain a neutral spine and avoid straining your neck.

Target muscles: Abdominals, hip flexors, and quadriceps

Purpose: Core strength, hip mobility, and lower body flexibility

Wall Supported Squats

Step-by-step directions:

1. Place your feet hip-width apart and slightly away from the wall as you stand with your back to the wall.

2. Put your arms out in front of you or at your sides.

3. Engage your core and slowly lower into a squat, sliding your back down the wall.

4. Keep your knees aligned with your ankles and avoid letting

5. Avoid letting your knees extend past your toes and keep them in line with your ankles.

6. Hold the squat position for 5–10 seconds, then slowly revert to the beginning position by sliding back up the wall.

Easier alternative: Do not lower into a full squat; instead, perform a shallow squat within a comfortable range of motion.

Expert advice: Throughout the exercise, keep your head, shoulders, and lower back in contact with the wall by distributing your weight evenly across your feet.

Target muscles: Quadriceps, hamstrings, glutes, and calves

Purpose: Lower body strength, balance, and muscle toning

Wall Leg Slides

Step-by-step directions:

1. Put your back to the wall while standing with your feet hip-width apart.

2. Activate your core and push the wall with your lower back.

3. Maintaining a bent and flexed knee, slowly glide your right foot up the wall.

4. Slide your foot back down and repeat on the left side.

Easier alternative: Slide your foot only partway up the wall, keeping the movement within a comfortable range of motion.

Expert advice: Maintain constant pressure between your lower back and the wall to ensure your core remains engaged.

Progression: Add ankle weights for added resistance or perform the exercise while holding a resistance band looped around your feet.

Target muscles: Abdominals, hip flexors, and quadriceps

Purpose: Core strength, pelvic stability, and hip mobility

Wall Hamstring Stretch

Target muscles: Hamstrings

Purpose: Flexibility and mobility

Step-by-step directions:

1. With your legs outstretched and your heels resting against the wall, lie on your back.

2. Engage your core and slowly slide your right heel up the wall, keeping your leg straight,

3. After 20–30 seconds of holding the stretch, slowly lower your right heel back down the wall.

4. Repeat for the left leg.

Easier alternative: Decrease the height of the leg lift or use a towel or resistance band to assist with the stretch.

Expert advice: Avoid overstretching the hamstring and pressing your lower back against the floor.

Wall Inner Thigh Squeeze

Target muscles: Inner thighs (adductors)

Purpose: Lower body strength and stability

1. Step-by-step directions:

2. Lie on your back with your legs extended and your heels resting against the wall.

3. Place a small pillow, soft ball, or folded towel between your knees.

4. Engage your core and press your lower back into the floor.

5. Squeeze the object between your knees for 2-3 seconds, then release slightly.

Easier alternative: Use a smaller or softer object between your knees or decrease the intensity of the squeeze.

Expert advice: Maintain contact between your lower back and the floor throughout the exercise.

Progression: Perform the exercise with your legs bent at a 90-degree angle, feet flat on the wall.

Wall Calf Raises

Target muscles: Calves

Purpose: Lower body strength and balance

Step-by-step directions:

1. Stand facing the wall, with your palms flat against the wall at shoulder height, and feet hip-width apart.

2. Engage your core and slowly raise your heels, coming onto your toes.

3. Hold the calf raise for 1-2 seconds, then slowly lower your heels back to the ground.

4. Repeat for 10-15 repetitions.

Easier alternative: Perform the exercise without the wall for support or decrease the height of the calf raise.

Expert advice: Maintain even weight distribution between the balls of your feet and your toes.

Wall-Assisted Lateral Leg Lifts

Target muscles: Outer thighs (abductors) and glutes

Purpose: Lower body strength and stability

Step-by-step directions:

1. Stand beside the wall with your left hand resting against the wall for support.

2. Engage your core and slowly lift your right leg to the side, keeping it straight.

3. Lower your right leg back down, maintaining control throughout the movement.

4. Repeat 10-15 repetitions on the right leg, then switch to the left.

Easier alternative: Decrease the height of the leg lift or perform the exercise with your knee slightly bent.

Expert advice: Keep your core engaged and avoid leaning too much into the wall for support.

PURPOSE-SPECIFIC EXERCISES

Welcome to the dynamic realm of Wall Pilates purpose-specific exercises, where innovation and practicality unite to redefine fitness boundaries. In this chapter, we'll explore the undeniable effectiveness of using a wall to enhance your Pilates routine, transforming your workout experience with targeted exercises that promote balance, strength, and flexibility. Say goodbye to complicated equipment and hello to results-driven training, as you unlock the potential of your body through this unique approach. Prepare to dive into the world of Wall Pilates and unlock a new level of fitness mastery that is as efficient as empowering.

Balance Exercises

Wall-Assisted Tree Pose

Target muscles: Core, hips, and lower leg stabilizers

Step-by-step directions:

1. Stand beside the wall with your right hand resting against the wall for support.

2. Shift your weight onto your right foot and bring your left foot to rest on your right ankle, calf, or inner thigh (avoid placing it directly on the knee).

3. Engage your core and maintain your balance, keeping your right hand on the wall for support.

4. Hold the position for 20-30 seconds, then switch sides.

Easier alternative: Keep your left toes resting on the ground with your heel on your right ankle.

Expert advice: Keep your hips square and avoid leaning into the wall.

Wall-Assisted Single Leg Deadlift

Target muscles: Hamstrings, glutes, and core

Step-by-step directions:

1. Stand facing the wall with your palms flat against the wall at shoulder height, and feet hip-width apart.

2. Engage your core and shift your weight onto your left foot.

3. Slowly hinge at the hips, lifting your right leg straight behind you and lowering your chest toward the wall.

4. Return to the starting position and repeat for 10-15 repetitions, then switch legs.

Easier alternative: Decrease the range of motion or keep your toes touching the ground for balance.

Expert advice: Maintain a neutral spine and avoid rounding your lower back.

Wall-Assisted Warrior III

Target muscles: Core, glutes, hamstrings, and shoulders

Step-by-step directions:

1. Stand facing the wall with your palms flat against the wall at shoulder height, and feet hip-width apart.

2. Engage your core and shift your weight onto your left foot.

3. Slowly lift your right leg behind you while keeping your upper body parallel to the floor.

4. Hold the position for 5-10 seconds, then return to the starting position.

5. Repeat for 5 repetitions, then switch legs.

Easier alternative: Keep your back toes resting on the ground with your heel lifted.

Expert advice: Maintain a neutral spine and avoid arching your lower back.

Wall-Assisted Figure Four Balance

Target muscles: Hips, glutes, and core

Step-by-step directions:

1. Stand facing the wall with your palms flat against the wall at shoulder height, and feet hip-width apart.

2. Engage your core and shift your weight onto your left foot.

3. Lift your right foot and place it on your left ankle, calf, or thigh (avoid placing it directly on the knee).

4. Hold the position for 20–30 seconds, then switch sides.

Easier alternative: Place your right foot on your left ankle with your toes touching the ground.

Expert advice: Keep your hips square and maintain even weight distribution on your standing foot.

Wall-Assisted Toe Taps

Target muscles: Core and lower leg stabilizers

Step-by-step directions:

Stand facing the wall with your palms flat against the wall at shoulder height, and feet hip-width apart.

Engage your core and slowly lift your right foot off the ground, tapping your toes to your left ankle.

Return your right foot to the ground and repeat with your left foot, tapping your toes to your right ankle.

Continue alternating sides for 10–15 repetitions on each side.

Easier alternative: Lift your feet only a few inches off the ground for balance assistance.

Expert advice: Keep your core engaged and maintain a tall posture throughout the exercise.

Flexibility Exercises

Wall Chest Stretch

Target muscles: Chest and shoulders

Step-by-step directions:

1. Stand facing the wall with your right arm extended to the side, palm flat against the wall at shoulder height.

2. Slowly turn your body to the left until you feel a stretch in your chest and shoulder.

3. Hold the stretch for 20–30 seconds, then switch sides.

Easier alternative: Bend your arm at a 90-degree angle to decrease the intensity of the stretch.

Expert advice: Keep your shoulders relaxed and avoid overstretching.

Wall-Assisted Hamstring Stretch

Target muscles: Hamstrings

Step-by-step directions:

1. Stand facing the wall with your right foot propped up against the wall, heel on the ground and toes pointing upward.

2. Keep your right leg straight and engage your core as you slowly hinge at the hips, bringing your chest toward your right knee.

3. Hold the stretch for 20–30 seconds, then switch legs.

Easier alternative: Decrease the height of your foot on the wall or bend your knee slightly.

Expert advice: Maintain a neutral spine and avoid rounding your lower back.

Wall-Assisted Quadriceps Stretch

Target muscles: Quadriceps

Step-by-step directions:

1. Stand facing away from the wall with your right foot slightly forward, and your left foot resting against the wall, toes pointing upward.

2. Bend your left knee and engage your core to maintain your balance.

3. Hold the stretch for 20-30 seconds, then switch legs.

Easier alternative: Hold onto a chair or other sturdy surface for balance assistance.

Expert advice: Keep your hips square and avoid arching your lower back.

Progression: Perform the stretch without the wall, grasping your foot with your hand.

Wall-Assisted Calf Stretch

Target muscles: Calves

Step-by-step directions:

1. Stand facing the wall with your palms flat against the wall at shoulder height.

2. Step your right foot back, keeping your heel on the ground and your right leg straight.

3. Engage your core and lean into the wall, keeping both feet flat.

4. Hold the stretch for 20-30 seconds, then switch legs.

Easier alternative: Decrease the distance between your feet or bend your back knee slightly.

Expert advice: Keep both feet flat and maintain an even weight distribution.

Wall-Assisted Hip Flexor Stretch

Target muscles: Hip flexors

Step-by-step directions:

1. Stand facing away from the wall, about two feet away from it.

2. Place your right foot against the wall, your toes pointing upward, and your left foot flat on the ground before you.

3. Engage your core and slowly bend your left knee, pressing your right knee into the wall.

4. Hold the stretch for 20-30 seconds, then switch legs.

Easier alternative: Decrease the height of your foot on the wall or bend your knee slightly.

Expert advice: Keep your hips square and avoid arching your lower back.

Posture Exercises

Wall Scapular Retraction

Target muscles: Upper back and shoulders

Step-by-step directions:

1. Stand facing the wall with your palms flat against the wall at shoulder height, and feet hip-width apart.

2. Engage your core and squeeze your shoulder blades together, pressing your chest toward the wall without bending your elbows.

3. Return to the starting position and repeat for 10-15 repetitions.

Easier alternative: Perform the exercise with your hands on a higher surface, like a countertop.

Expert advice: Keep your neck relaxed and avoid shrugging your shoulders.

Wall-Assisted Neck Stretch

Target muscles: Neck and upper back

Step-by-step directions:

Stand facing the wall with your right palm flat against the wall at shoulder height.

Tilt your head to the left, bringing your left ear toward your left shoulder.

Hold the stretch for 20–30 seconds, then switch sides.

Easier alternative: Decrease the intensity of the stretch by not tilting your head as far.

Expert advice: Keep your shoulders relaxed and avoid overstretching.

Wall T-Spine Rotation

Target muscles: Thoracic spine, shoulders, and chest

Step-by-step directions:

1. Stand with your right side against the wall, feet hip-width apart, and knees slightly bent.

2. Place your right hand on your left shoulder and your left hand on the wall for support.

3. Engage your core and slowly rotate your upper body to the left, opening your chest and extending your left arm to the side.

4. Return to the starting position and repeat for 10–15 repetitions, then switch sides.

Easier alternative: Decrease the range of motion or perform the exercise with your hand on a higher surface, like a countertop.

Expert advice: Keep your hips square and avoid twisting your lower back.

Wall-Assisted Hip Hinge

Target muscles: Hamstrings, glutes, and lower back

Step-by-step directions:

1. Stand with your back against the wall, feet hip-width apart, and about 6 inches from the wall.

2. Engage your core, and slowly hinge forward at the hips with a slight bend in your knees while maintaining contact with the wall using your glutes and lower back.

3. Return to the starting position by pushing your hips against the wall and straightening your upper body.

4. Repeat for 10-15 repetitions.

Easier alternative: Decrease the range of motion or perform the exercise with your feet closer to the wall.

Expert advice: Maintain a neutral spine throughout the movement and avoid rounding your lower back.

Wall-Assisted Pelvic Tilt

Target muscles: Core, lower back, and glutes

Step-by-step directions:

1. Stand with your back against the wall, feet hip-width apart, and knees slightly bent.

2. Engage your core and press your lower back against the wall by tucking your pelvis under.

3. Slowly return to the starting position, maintaining contact with the wall.

4. Repeat for 10-15 repetitions.

Easier alternative: Decrease the range of motion or perform the exercise while seated on a stability ball or chair.

Expert advice: Focus on using your core muscles to initiate the movement and avoid overarching your lower back.

Coordination Exercises

Wall Tap March

Target muscles: Core, hip flexors, and quads

Step-by-step directions:

1. Stand with your back against the wall, feet hip-width apart, and hands resting on your hips.

2. Engage your core and slowly lift your right knee to tap the wall before you.

3. Lower your right foot and repeat with your left knee.

4. Continue alternating legs for 10-15 repetitions on each side.

Easier alternative: Decrease the height of the knee lifts or perform the exercise while seated on a chair.

Expert advice: Maintain a tall posture and engage your core throughout the movement.

Wall-Assisted Leg Swings

Target muscles: Core, hip flexors, and glutes

Step-by-step directions:

1. Stand facing the wall with your left hand on the wall for support, and your right hand on your hip.

2. Engage your core and slowly swing your right leg forward and backward in a controlled motion.

3. Repeat for 10-15 repetitions, then switch legs.

Easier alternative: Decrease the range of motion or perform the exercise with your leg bent at the knee.

Expert advice: Maintain a tall posture and avoid leaning forward or backward during the movement.

Wall-Assisted Arm Circles

Target muscles: Shoulders, chest, and upper back

Step-by-step directions:

1. Stand with your right side against the wall, feet hip-width apart, and your right arm extended to the side at shoulder height.

2. Engage your core and make small circles with your right arm, maintaining contact with the wall.

3. Perform 10-15 repetitions in each direction, then switch sides.

Easier alternative: Perform the exercise with your arm in a lower position or decrease the size of the circles.

Expert advice: Keep your shoulders relaxed and avoid shrugging.

Wall Heel Raises with Toe Taps

Target muscles: Calves, core, and coordination

Step-by-step directions:

1. Stand with your back against the wall, feet hip-width apart, and hands resting on your hips.

2. Engage your core and slowly raise your heels off the ground while tapping your right toes against the wall.

3. Lower your heels and right foot, then repeat on the left side.

4. Continue alternating sides for 10-15 repetitions on each side.

Easier alternative: Perform the exercise without the toe taps or do heel raises and toe taps separately.

Expert advice: Maintain a tall posture and engage your core throughout the movement.

Wall Cross-Tap

Target muscles: Core, shoulders, and coordination

Step-by-step directions:

1. Stand facing the wall with your arms extended in front of you, palms touching the wall.

2. Engage your core and slowly slide your right hand across your body to touch your left shoulder.

3. Return your right hand to the starting position and repeat with your left hand, sliding it across to touch your right shoulder.

4. Continue alternating hands for 10–15 repetitions on each side.

Easier alternative: Perform the exercise with your hands on a higher surface, like a countertop.

Expert advice: Keep your core engaged and maintain a neutral spine throughout the movement.

BOOK 3: THE WORKOUT PLAN

INTRODUCTION

Welcome to the Wall Pilates Workout Book, your ultimate guide to unlocking the incredible benefits of wall Pilates through a comprehensive 28-Day Challenge! Designed with beginners in mind, this book is packed with various easy-to-follow, low-impact workouts that will help you achieve greater flexibility, strength, balance, and overall well-being. Inside these pages, you'll discover a diverse range of workouts, including:

- 5-Minute Power Workout

- The Upper Body Blast

- Wall Pilates Core Crusher

- Lower Body Sculptor

- Wall Pilates Full Body Fusion

- The Flexibility Boost

- The Balance Basics Workout

- Posture Perfection Workout

- The Radiant Workout

Embark on the 28-Day Wall Pilates Challenge, which takes you on a progressive journey through daily workouts and wellness practices, providing an engaging and comprehensive experience. Each day of the challenge is thoughtfully laid out, with clear instructions and guidance to help you maximize your results. Read the inspiring testimonials from individuals who have completed the challenge and experienced the transformative power of wall Pilates in their lives. Their stories serve as motivation and proof of the effectiveness of this program.

Get ready to discover the incredible benefits of wall Pilates and join the countless others who have transformed their lives through this amazing 28-Day Challenge. Your journey towards a healthier, happier, and more vibrant life starts now!

WALL PILATES WORKOUTS FOR BEGINNERS

5-Minute Power Workout

This full-body workout features exercises targeting the upper, core, and lower body. It only takes 5 minutes to complete, making it perfect for busy schedules or those new to Pilates. Perform each exercise for 30 seconds, and complete the entire circuit twice for 5 minutes.

Wall Push-ups (Upper Body)

● Stand facing the wall, placing your hands slightly wider than shoulder-width apart on the wall.

● Move your feet back to create an angle with your body.

● Lower your body towards the wall, bending your elbows.

● Push back to the starting position, straightening your arms.

- Perform for 30 seconds.

Wall Supported Dead Bug (Core)

- Lie on your back with your feet flat against the wall and knees bent at a 90-degree angle.

- Place your arms straight up towards the ceiling.

- Slowly lower your right arm and left leg down towards the floor, while keeping your other limbs in place.

- Return to the starting position and repeat with your left arm and right leg.

- Perform for 30 seconds.

Wall Supported Squats (Lower Body)

- Stand with your back against the wall and feet hip-width apart.

- Lower your body into a squat position, ensuring your knees do not extend past your toes.

- Hold for a few seconds before rising back up to the starting position.

- Perform for 30 seconds.

Wall Angels (Upper Body)

- Stand with your back against the wall and feet shoulder-width apart.

- Place your arms against the wall, elbows bent at a 90-degree angle and palms facing out.

- Slowly slide your arms up the wall, straightening them as you go.

- Slide your arms back down to the starting position.

- Perform for 30 seconds.

Wall Bridge (Core)

- Lie on your back with your knees bent and feet flat on the floor.

- Place your arms at your sides, palms facing down.

- Press your feet into the floor and lift your hips towards the ceiling.

- Hold for a few seconds before lowering back down.

- Perform for 30 seconds.

Wall Calf Raises (Lower Body)

- Stand facing the wall, placing your hands on the wall for support.

- Slowly raise your heels off the ground, balancing on the balls of your feet.

- Lower your heels back down to the floor.

- Perform for 30 seconds.

Complete the entire circuit twice for a total of 5 minutes. This workout is a quick and effective way to engage your full body, improve strength, and increase flexibility while using the wall for support.

The Upper Body Blast

This beginner-friendly upper body workout features exercises that target various muscle groups in the upper body. Perform each exercise for 10-15 repetitions and complete the entire circuit 2-3 times for 2-3 sets.

Wall Push-ups

- Stand facing the wall, placing your hands slightly wider than shoulder-width apart on the wall.

- Move your feet back to create an angle with your body.

- Lower your body towards the wall, bending your elbows.

- Push back to the starting position, straightening your arms.

- Perform for 10-15 repetitions.

Wall Angels

- Stand with your back against the wall and feet shoulder-width apart.

- Place your arms against the wall, elbows bent at a 90-degree angle and palms facing out.

- Slowly slide your arms up the wall, straightening them as you go.

- Slide your arms back down to the starting position.

- Perform for 10-15 repetitions.

Wall Tricep Dips

- Stand with your back to the wall and place your hands on the wall behind you, fingers pointing down.
- Bend your knees and lower your body by bending your elbows.
- Press into the wall to straighten your arms and return to the starting position.
- Perform for 10-15 repetitions.

Wall Bicep Curl

- Stand facing the wall, arms extended and hands shoulder-width apart on the wall.
- Bend your elbows and bring your face closer to the wall, as if you were curling your arms.
- Slowly extend your arms back to the starting position.
- Perform for 10-15 repetitions.

Wall Rows

- Stand facing the wall, arms extended and hands shoulder-width apart on the wall.
- Lean back slightly and engage your core.
- Pull your chest towards the wall by bending your elbows and squeezing your shoulder blades together.
- Slowly extend your arms back to the starting position.
- Perform for 10-15 repetitions.

Complete the entire circuit 2-3 times for 2-3 sets. This workout is a great way to strengthen and tone the upper body, using the wall for support and added resistance.

Wall Pilates Core Crusher

This beginner-friendly core workout features exercises that specifically target the core muscles. Perform each exercise for 10-15 repetitions (or hold for 30 seconds for static exercises) and complete the entire circuit 2-3 times for 2-3 sets.

Wall Roll Down

- Stand with your back against the wall and feet hip-width apart.

- Slowly roll down, peeling your spine away from the wall one vertebra at a time.

- Roll back up to the starting position, engaging your core.

- Perform for 10-15 repetitions.

Wall Plank

- Get into a plank position with your hands on the floor and feet against the wall.

- Engage your core and keep your body in a straight line.

- Hold for 30 seconds.

Wall Supported Dead Bug

- Lie on your back with your feet flat against the wall and knees bent at a 90-degree angle.

- Place your arms straight up towards the ceiling.

- Slowly lower your right arm and left leg down towards the floor, while keeping your other limbs in place.

- Return to the starting position and repeat with your left arm and right leg.

- Perform for 10-15 repetitions.

Wall Assisted Bicycle Crunch

- Lie on your back with your feet flat against the wall and knees bent at a 90-degree angle.

- Place your hands behind your head and lift your head and shoulders off the floor.

- Bring your right elbow towards your left knee while keeping your right foot against the wall.

- Switch sides, bringing your left elbow towards your right knee.

- Perform for 10-15 repetitions.

Wall Bridge

- Lie on your back with your knees bent and feet flat on the floor.

- Place your arms at your sides, palms facing down.

- Press your feet into the floor and lift your hips towards the ceiling.

- Hold for a few seconds before lowering back down.

- Perform for 10-15 repetitions.

Lower Body Sculptor

This beginner-friendly lower body workout features exercises that target various muscle groups in the lower body. Perform each exercise for 10-15 repetitions and complete the entire circuit 2-3 times for 2-3 sets.

Wall Pelvic Curl

- Lie on your back with your knees bent and feet flat on the floor.

- Place your arms at your sides, palms facing down.

- Press your feet into the floor and lift your hips towards the ceiling while curling your pelvis.

- Slowly lower back down to the starting position.

- Perform for 10-15 repetitions.

Wall Supported Clamshells

- Lie on your side with your back against the wall, knees bent, and feet together.

- Keeping your feet touching, open your top knee away from the bottom knee.

- Slowly close your knees back together.

- Perform for 10-15 repetitions, then switch sides.

Wall Supported Scissor Kicks

- Lie on your back with your legs extended up and feet flat against the wall.

- Keeping your legs straight, lower one leg towards the floor.

- Raise the lowered leg back to the wall as you lower the opposite leg.

- Perform for 10-15 repetitions.

Wall Supported Squats

- Stand with your back against the wall and feet hip-width apart.

- Lower your body into a squat position, ensuring your knees do not extend past your toes.

- Hold for a few seconds before rising back up to the starting position.

- Perform for 10-15 repetitions.

Wall Inner Thigh Squeeze

- Stand with your back against the wall, feet hip-width apart, and place a soft ball or pillow between your knees.

- Engage your core and press your knees together, squeezing the ball or pillow.

- Hold for a few seconds, then release the pressure.

- Perform for 10-15 repetitions.

Wall Calf Raises

- Stand facing the wall, placing your hands on the wall for support.

- Slowly raise your heels off the ground, balancing on the balls of your feet.

- Lower your heels back down to the floor.

- Perform for 10-15 repetitions.

Wall Pilates Full Body Fusion

This beginner-friendly full body workout features exercises that target various muscle groups in the upper body, core, and lower body. Perform each exercise for 10-15 repetitions and complete the entire circuit 2-3 times for 2-3 sets.

Wall Push-ups:

- Stand facing the wall with your hands at shoulder height and slightly wider than shoulder-width apart.

- Bend your elbows and lower your body towards the wall.

- Push back to the starting position.

- Perform 10-15 repetitions.

Wall Rows:

- Stand facing the wall with your arms extended and hands placed on the wall.
- Lean back slightly, keeping your body straight.
- Pull your chest towards the wall, bending your elbows.
- Extend your arms back to the starting position.
- Perform 10-15 repetitions.

Wall Shoulder Press:

- Stand with your back against the wall, arms extended overhead.
- Bend your elbows and lower your hands down to your shoulders.
- Press your hands back up, extending your arms fully.
- Perform 10-15 repetitions.

Wall Roll Down:

- Stand with your back against the wall, feet hip-width apart.
- Roll your spine down the wall, one vertebra at a time, until your hands touch the floor or as low as you can comfortably go.
- Roll back up slowly to the starting position.
- Perform 10-15 repetitions.

Wall Plank:

- Face the wall and place your hands on the wall, shoulder-width apart.
- Step back until your body is straight from head to heels.
- Hold this position for 30 seconds.

Wall Supported Squats:

- Stand with your back against the wall and feet hip-width apart.
- Lower your body into a squat position, ensuring your knees do not extend past your toes.
- Hold for a few seconds before rising back up to the starting position.
- Perform 10-15 repetitions.

Wall Hamstring Stretch:

- Stand facing the wall with one heel resting against the wall and the other foot flat on the floor.

- Keeping your legs straight, hinge at your hips, and reach your hands towards your toes.

- Hold the stretch for 15-20 seconds per leg.

Wall Calf Raises:

- Stand facing the wall, placing your hands on the wall for support.

- Slowly raise your heels off the ground, balancing on the balls of your feet.

- Lower your heels back down to the floor.

- Perform 10-15 repetitions.

The Flexibility Boost

This beginner-friendly flexibility workout features exercises that target various muscle groups to improve overall flexibility and range of motion. Perform each exercise for the recommended duration, focusing on a gentle stretch without overextending. Complete the entire circuit 1-2 times for 1-2 sets.

Wall Chest Stretch:

● Stand next to a wall with your arm extended out to the side and your palm against the wall.

● Slowly rotate your body away from the wall until you feel a gentle stretch across your chest.

● Hold the stretch for 15-20 seconds.

● Repeat on the other side.

Wall-Assisted Hamstring Stretch:

● Stand facing the wall with one heel resting against the wall and the other foot flat on the floor.

● Keeping your legs straight, hinge at your hips, and reach your hands towards your toes.

● Hold the stretch for 15-20 seconds per leg.

Wall-Assisted Quadriceps Stretch:

● Stand facing away from the wall, placing one foot against the wall with your knee bent.

● Hold onto a sturdy object for balance if needed.

● Gently press your hips forward to feel a stretch in your quadriceps.

● Hold the stretch for 15-20 seconds per leg.

Wall-Assisted Calf Stretch:

● Stand facing the wall with your hands on the wall for support.

● Place one foot behind the other, keeping both feet flat on the ground.

● Lean into the wall until you feel a stretch in the calf of the back leg.

● Hold the stretch for 15-20 seconds per leg.

Wall-Assisted Hip Flexor Stretch:

- Stand facing away from the wall, placing the top of your foot against the wall with your knee bent.

- Gently press your hips forward to feel a stretch in the front of your hip.

- Hold the stretch for 15-20 seconds per leg.

The Balance Basics Workout

This beginner-friendly balance workout features exercises that target various muscle groups to improve overall balance, stability, and coordination. Perform each exercise for the recommended repetitions, focusing on maintaining control and balance. Complete the entire circuit 1-2 times for 1-2 sets.

Wall-Assisted Tree Pose:

- Stand next to a wall with your hand on the wall for support.

- Shift your weight to one leg and place the sole of the opposite foot on the inner thigh or calf of the standing leg.

- Hold the pose for 15-20 seconds per leg.

Wall-Assisted Single Leg Deadlift:

- Stand facing the wall with your hands on the wall for support.

- Shift your weight to one leg and slowly hinge at the hips, lifting the other leg behind you.

- Lower your torso and leg until they are parallel to the ground.

- Slowly return to the starting position.

- Perform 8-10 repetitions per leg.

Wall-Assisted Warrior III:

- Stand facing the wall with your hands on the wall for support.

- Shift your weight to one leg and extend the other leg behind you.

- Slowly lift your back leg while keeping your hands on the wall, hinging at the hips until your torso and back leg are parallel to the ground.

- Hold the pose for 10-15 seconds per leg.

Wall-Assisted Figure Four Balance:

- Stand next to a wall with your hand on the wall for support.

- Shift your weight to one leg and place the ankle of the opposite leg above the knee of the standing leg.

- Gently bend your standing leg, creating a figure-four shape with your legs.

- Hold the pose for 15-20 seconds per leg.

Wall-Assisted Toe Taps:

- Stand facing the wall with your hands on the wall for support.

- Shift your weight to one leg and the other to the side.

- Tap your toes on the ground, keeping your weight on the standing leg.

- Perform 10-12 repetitions per leg.

Posture Perfection Workout

This beginner-friendly posture workout features exercises that target various muscle groups to improve overall posture, body alignment, and muscle balance. Perform each exercise for the recommended repetitions, focusing on maintaining proper form and alignment. Complete the entire circuit 1-2 times for 1-2 sets.

Wall Scapular Retraction:

- Stand with your back against a wall.

- Place your arms at a 90-degree angle, elbows touching the wall.

- Squeeze your shoulder blades together, bringing your elbows closer to each other.

- Hold for 2-3 seconds and release.

- Perform 10-12 repetitions.

Wall-Assisted Neck Stretch:

- Stand with your back against a wall.

- Tilt your head to one side, bringing your ear towards your shoulder.

- Use your hand to press your head down for a deeper stretch gently.

- Hold for 15-20 seconds per side.

Wall T-Spine Rotation:

- Stand with your side against a wall, feet hip-width apart.

- Place one hand on the wall and the other on your hip.

- Rotate your torso, reaching the hand on your hip towards the wall.

- Return to the starting position.

- Perform 8-10 repetitions per side.

Wall-Assisted Hip Hinge:

- Stand facing the wall with your feet hip-width apart and toes touching the wall.

- Place your hands on your hips.

- Hinge at the hips, keeping a slight bend in your knees and lowering your torso towards the wall.

- Keep your back straight and return to the starting position.

- Perform 10-12 repetitions.

Wall-Assisted Pelvic Tilt:

- Stand with your back against a wall.

- Place your hands on your hips.

- Tuck your pelvis under, flattening your lower back against the wall.

- Release and return to the starting position.

- Perform 10-12 repetitions.

The Radiant Workout

This beginner-friendly wall Pilates workout focuses on improving general well-being, including mobility, flexibility, and muscle activation. Perform each exercise for the recommended repetitions and sets, maintaining proper form and alignment. Complete the entire circuit 1-2 times for 1-2 sets.

Wall Tap March:

- Stand facing the wall, arms extended and hands resting on the wall.

- March in place, lifting each knee to tap the wall.

- Perform for 30 seconds.

Wall-Assisted Leg Swings:

- Stand facing the wall, with one hand on the wall for support.

- Swing one leg forward and backward, keeping it straight.

- Perform 10-12 swings per leg.

Wall-Assisted Arm Circles:

- Stand with your back against the wall.

- Extend your arms to the sides at shoulder height, palms facing down.

- Make small circles with your arms, keeping them in contact with the wall.

- Perform 10-12 circles in each direction.

Wall Heel Raises with Toe Taps:

- Stand facing the wall, with your hands on the wall for support.

- Raise your heels off the ground, then lower them back down.

- Tap your right toes to the side and return to the starting position.

- Repeat with the left toes.

- Perform 10-12 repetitions per side.

Wall Cross-Tap:

- Stand with your back against the wall, feet hip-width apart.

- Lift your right leg and tap your left hand to your right foot.

- Return to the starting position and repeat on the other side.

- Perform 10-12 repetitions per side.

6-10. Stretching exercises:

Perform each stretching exercise for 15-30 seconds, focusing on breathing and relaxation.

- Wall Chest Stretch

- Wall-Assisted Hamstring Stretch

- Wall-Assisted Quadriceps Stretch

- Wall-Assisted Calf Stretch

- Wall-Assisted Hip Flexor Stretch

Complete the entire circuit 1-2 times for 1-2 sets. This workout is a great way to enhance your overall well-being, using the wall for support and guidance. Listen to your body and modify necessary exercises to ensure safety and effectiveness.

THE 28-DAY WALL PILATES CHALLENGE

Welcome to the 28-Day Wall Pilates Challenge – an exciting and transformative journey to enhance vitality, flexibility, posture, and energy levels! This beginner-friendly program is perfect for everyone, regardless of age, gender, or fitness level. Whether you're a busy professional, a stay-at-home parent, a senior, or just starting your fitness journey, this challenge suits your needs and provides steady, progressive improvement.

In just 10 minutes a day, you'll experience the powerful benefits of wall Pilates as you work through our carefully curated series of low-impact exercises. The wall provides excellent support, stability, and guidance, ensuring proper alignment and technique while minimizing the risk of injury. With each day of the challenge, you'll notice the positive effects on your overall well-being as your flexibility, balance, and strength improve.

Throughout the 28 days, we will guide you through various engaging workouts and share valuable wellness practices to enhance your physical health and well-being. This holistic approach ensures that you care for your body inside and out, setting the stage for long-lasting, sustainable results.

So, are you ready to unlock your full potential and experience the benefits of the 28-Day Wall Pilates Challenge? Join us today and embark on an empowering journey towards a healthier, happier, and more energetic you!

Day #1: Welcome to the 28-Day Wall Pilates Challenge!

Kick-off this challenge with enthusiasm! Enjoy the journey to greater flexibility, strength, and balance.

Warm-up:

- 2 minutes of marching in place
- 2 minutes of shoulder rolls
- 1 minute of knee lifts

Workout:

- 1 minute of wall push-ups
- 1 minute of wall squats
- 1 minute of wall slides
- 1 minute of wall leg lifts (30 seconds each leg)
- 1 minute of wall plank

Cool down:

- 1 minute of deep breathing
- 2 minutes of standing forward fold
- 2 minutes of chest and shoulder stretch against the wall

Wellness practice: 5 minutes of mindfulness meditation. Find a quiet place, sit comfortably, and focus on your breath. Whenever your mind wanders, gently bring it back to your breath.

Day #2: Strengthen Your Core!

Today, we'll focus on strengthening your core muscles. A strong core will improve your balance and overall fitness.

Warm-up:

- 2 minutes of step-touches

- 2 minutes of arm circles

- 1 minute of hip circles

Workout:

- 1 minute of wall push-ups with alternating shoulder taps

- 1 minute of wall squats with alternating heel raises

- 1 minute of wall mountain climbers

- 1 minute of wall leg circles (30 seconds each leg)

- 1 minute of wall plank knee tucks

Cool down:

- 1 minute of deep breathing

- 2 minutes of standing quad stretch

- 2 minutes of wall-assisted hamstring stretch

Wellness practice: Pay attention to your posture throughout the day, especially while sitting or standing for extended periods. Proper posture can help prevent back pain, improve breathing, and reduce muscle fatigue.

Day #3: Find Your Balance!

Today, we'll focus on balance exercises to help improve your stability and coordination.

Warm-up:

- 2 minutes of side-to-side toe taps

- 2 minutes of wrist circles

- 1 minute of ankle circles

Workout:

- 1 minute of wall-assisted single-leg stance (30 seconds each leg)

- 1 minute of wall-assisted leg swings (30 seconds each leg)

- 1 minute of wall-assisted tree pose (30 seconds each leg)

- 1 minute of wall-assisted side leg lifts (30 seconds each leg)

- 1 minute of wall-assisted arabesque (30 seconds each leg)

Cool down:

- 1 minute of deep breathing

- 2 minutes of standing forward fold with a twist

- 2 minutes of wall-assisted calf stretch

Wellness practice: Drink at least 8 cups of water today. Staying hydrated helps maintain overall health and energy levels.

Day #4: Upper Body Strength!

Today, we'll focus on strengthening your upper body, essential for good posture and everyday activities.

Warm-up:

- 2 minutes of gentle jogging in place

- 2 minutes of neck stretches

- 1 minute of side bends

Workout:

- 1 minute of wall push-ups with a wide hand position

- 1 minute of wall tricep dips

- 1 minute of wall plank shoulder taps

- 1 minute of wall-supported side plank (30 seconds each side)

- 1 minute of wall-assisted superman

Cool down:

- 1 minute of deep breathing

- 2 minutes of wall-assisted chest stretch

- 2 minutes of wall-assisted tricep stretch

Wellness practice: Take a 10-minute walk outside. Fresh air and a little movement will boost your mood and energy levels.

Day #5: Lengthen and Strengthen!

Today, we'll focus on exercises that strengthen your muscles, promoting flexibility and muscle tone.

Warm-up:

- 2 minutes of gentle high knees

- 2 minutes of shoulder shrugs

- 1 minute of standing side stretches

Workout:

- 1 minute of wall push-ups with a narrow hand position

- 1 minute of wall-assisted single-leg deadlifts (30 seconds each leg)

- 1 minute of wall-assisted leg extensions (30 seconds each leg)

- 1 minute of wall-assisted side plank with leg lift (30 seconds each side)

- 1 minute of wall-assisted back extensions

Cool down:

- 1 minute of deep breathing

- 2 minutes of wall-assisted chest stretch

- 2 minutes of wall-assisted shoulder stretch

Wellness practice: Spend 10 minutes in mindful silence. Turn off distractions and tune into your thoughts and emotions, observing them without judgment.

Day #6: Dynamic Moves!

Today, we'll focus on dynamic movements that increase your heart rate and challenge your muscles.

Warm-up:

- 2 minutes of gentle jumping jacks

- 2 minutes of arm swings

- 1 minute of gentle spinal twists

Workout:

- 1 minute of wall push-ups with leg lift (30 seconds each leg)

- 1 minute of wall-assisted jump squats

- 1 minute of wall plank with alternating toe taps

- 1 minute of wall-assisted alternating lunges

- 1 minute of wall mountain climbers

Cool down:

- 1 minute of deep breathing

- 2 minutes of wall-assisted figure four stretch

- 2 minutes of wall-assisted lateral side stretch

Wellness practice: Write a short list of personal strengths and achievements. Acknowledging your accomplishments can boost self-esteem and motivation.

Day #7: Active Recovery!

Today, let's focus on stretching and recovery to help your muscles rejuvenate and prepare for the coming week.

Warm-up:

- 2 minutes of gentle toe taps

- 2 minutes of neck and shoulder rolls

- 1 minute of ankle rolls

Workout:

- 1 minute of wall-assisted forward fold

- 1 minute of wall-assisted downward dog

- 1 minute of wall-assisted child's pose

- 1 minute of wall-assisted cobra pose

- 1 minute of wall-assisted cat-cow stretch

Cool down:

- 1 minute of deep breathing

- 2 minutes of wall-assisted quad stretch

- 2 minutes of wall-assisted seated forward fold

Wellness practice: Engage in outdoor activities, such as hiking, cycling, or swimming, to benefit from the combination of physical activity and exposure to nature. Spending time outdoors can improve mood, increase vitamin D levels, and promote well-being.

Day 8: Core Power!

Let's focus on enhancing your core stability and strength, essential for good posture and daily activities.

Warm-up:

- 2 minutes of gentle side-to-side steps
- 2 minutes of wrist rolls
- 1 minute of standing hip circles

Workout:

- 1 minute of wall plank with alternating knee tucks
- 1 minute of wall-assisted bicycle crunches
- 1 minute of wall-assisted Russian twists
- 1 minute of wall-supported dead bug
- 1 minute of wall-assisted plank jacks

Cool down:

- 1 minute of deep breathing
- 2 minutes of wall-assisted standing forward fold
- 2 minutes of wall-assisted pigeon pose

Wellness practice: Unplug for 30 minutes. Turn off your electronic devices and engage in a mindful activity like journaling or meditation.

Day 9: Balance Boost!

Improve your balance and coordination with today's exercises, supporting your fitness.

Warm-up:

- 2 minutes of gentle heel raises
- 2 minutes of shoulder circles
- 1 minute of knee lifts

Workout:

- 1 minute of wall-assisted single-leg squats (30 seconds each leg)
- 1 minute of wall-assisted single-leg calf raises (30 seconds each leg)
- 1 minute of wall-assisted warrior III (30 seconds each leg)
- 1 minute of wall-assisted side plank with leg lift (30 seconds each side)
- 1 minute of wall-assisted half-moon pose (30 seconds each side)

Cool down:

- 1 minute of deep breathing
- 2 minutes of wall-assisted seated forward fold
- 2 minutes of wall-assisted butterfly stretch

Wellness practice: Write a positive affirmation and repeat it throughout the day. Positive affirmations can boost self-esteem and motivation.

Day #10: Lower Body Strength!

Focus on strengthening your lower body, essential for mobility and overall muscle balance.

Warm-up:

- 2 minutes of gentle side shuffles

- 2 minutes of ankle circles

- 1 minute of hip circles

Workout:

- 1 minute of wall squats with calf raises

- 1 minute of wall-assisted reverse lunges (30 seconds each leg)

- 1 minute of wall-assisted glute bridges

- 1 minute of wall-assisted side-lying leg lifts (30 seconds each leg)

- 1 minute of wall-assisted single-leg hamstring curls (30 seconds each leg)

Cool down:

- 1 minute of deep breathing

- 2 minutes of wall-assisted figure four stretch

- 2 minutes of wall-assisted standing hamstring stretch

Wellness practice: Spend 5 minutes practicing deep breathing exercises. Inhale deeply through your nose for a count of 4, then exhale slowly through your mouth for a count of 6.

Day #11: Full Body Fusion!

Today, we'll combine upper, lower, and core exercises for a full-body workout.

Warm-up:

- 2 minutes of gentle high knees

- 2 minutes of arm swings

- 1 minute of gentle spinal twists

Workout:

- 1 minute of wall push-ups with alternating leg lifts

- 1 minute of wall-assisted squat with side leg lift

- 1 minute of wall-assisted plank with shoulder tap

- 1 minute of wall-assisted curtsy lunges (30 seconds each leg)

- 1 minute of wall-assisted seated Russian twists

Cool down:

- 1 minute of deep breathing

- 2 minutes of wall-assisted chest stretch

- 2 minutes of wall-assisted calf stretch

Wellness practice: Set a small, achievable goal for the day and follow through with it. Achieving daily goals can boost self-esteem and motivation.

Day 12: Stretch and Recover!

Let's focus on flexibility and recovery with gentle stretches to prepare your body for the coming days.

Warm-up:

- 2 minutes of gentle toe taps

- 2 minutes of shoulder rolls

- 1 minute of standing side stretches

Workout:

- 1 minute of wall-assisted forward fold

- 1 minute of wall-assisted downward dog

- 1 minute of wall-assisted triangle pose (30 seconds each side)

- 1 minute of wall-assisted seated wide-leg forward fold

- 1 minute of wall-assisted seated twist (30 seconds each side)

Cool down:

- 1 minute of deep breathing

- 2 minutes of wall-assisted butterfly stretch

- 2 minutes of wall-assisted reclined twist (1 minute each side)

Wellness practice: Spend 10 minutes in nature. Take a walk in the park or sit outside to enjoy the fresh air and the calming effects of nature.

Day 13: Core Challenge!

Strengthen your core muscles for better posture and overall fitness.

Warm-up:

- 2 minutes of gentle step-touches

- 2 minutes of wrist circles

- 1 minute of hip circles

Workout:

- 1 minute of wall-assisted plank with alternating leg lifts

- 1 minute of wall-assisted seated leg lifts

- 1 minute of wall-assisted superman with opposite arm and leg lift

- 1 minute of wall-assisted seated bicycle crunches

- 1 minute of wall-assisted side plank dips (30 seconds each side)

Cool down:

- 1 minute of deep breathing

- 2 minutes of wall-assisted standing forward fold

- 2 minutes of wall-assisted pigeon pose

Wellness practice: Schedule short, active breaks throughout your day, such as a 5-minute walk or a quick set of bodyweight exercises. This can help combat the negative effects of prolonged sitting and boost energy levels.

Day 14: Balance and Coordination!

Improve your balance and coordination with today's workout!

Warm-up:

- 2 minutes of gentle marching in place

- 2 minutes of arm circles

- 1 minute of knee lifts

Workout:

- 1 minute of wall-assisted single-leg squats (30 seconds each leg)

- 1 minute of wall-assisted single-leg reaches (30 seconds each leg)

- 1 minute of wall-assisted warrior II (30 seconds each side)

- 1 minute of wall-assisted side plank with arm extension (30 seconds each side)

- 1 minute of wall-assisted single-leg hip hinges (30 seconds each leg)

Cool down:

- 1 minute of deep breathing

- 2 minutes of wall-assisted seated forward fold

- 2 minutes of wall-assisted butterfly stretch

Day 15: Upper Body Power!

Strengthen your upper body for better posture and ease in daily activities.

Warm-up:

- 2 minutes of gentle jogging in place

- 2 minutes of neck stretches

- 1 minute of side bends

Workout:

- 1 minute of wall push-ups with hands at shoulder-width

- 1 minute of wall tricep push-ups

- 1 minute of wall plank to push-up

- 1 minute of wall-assisted T-plank (30 seconds each side)

- 1 minute of wall-assisted Y-raises

Cool down:

- 1 minute of deep breathing

- 2 minutes of wall-assisted chest stretch

- 2 minutes of wall-assisted tricep stretch

Wellness practice: Spend 10 minutes visualizing a positive future outcome. Visualization can increase motivation and help you work towards your goals.

Day 16: Lower Body Burn!

Focus on building strength and endurance in your lower body.

Warm-up:

- 2 minutes of gentle side shuffles

- 2 minutes of ankle circles

- 1 minute of hip circles

Workout:

- 1 minute of wall squats with alternating toe taps

- 1 minute of wall-assisted lateral lunges (30 seconds each leg)

- 1 minute of wall-assisted glute bridge march

- 1 minute of wall-assisted standing leg circles (30 seconds each leg)

- 1 minute of wall-assisted single-leg Romanian deadlifts (30 seconds each leg)

Cool down:

- 1 minute of deep breathing

- 2 minutes of wall-assisted figure four stretch

- 2 minutes of wall-assisted standing hamstring stretch

Wellness practice: Write a list of 3 things you're grateful for. Practicing gratitude can improve mental well-being, reduce stress, and promote positive emotions. Make it a daily habit to reflect on the positive aspects of your life.

Day 17: Flexibility Flow!

Today, focus on enhancing your flexibility and range of motion with fluid movements.

Warm-up:

- 2 minutes of gentle high knees

- 2 minutes of shoulder rolls

- 1 minute of gentle spinal twists

Workout:

- 1 minute of wall-assisted standing cat-cow stretch

- 1 minute of wall-assisted side bend stretch (30 seconds each side)

- 1 minute of wall-assisted seated wide-leg forward fold

- 1 minute of wall-assisted seated twist (30 seconds each side)

- 1 minute of wall-assisted thread-the-needle pose (30 seconds each side)

Cool down:

- 1 minute of deep breathing
- 2 minutes of wall-assisted standing forward fold
- 2 minutes of wall-assisted calf stretch

Wellness practice: Spend 10 minutes stretching or practicing gentle yoga poses before bedtime. This can help calm your body and mind, promoting a better night's sleep.

Day 18: Core Stability!

Enhance your core strength for improved balance and daily function.

Warm-up:

- 2 minutes of gentle side-to-side steps
- 2 minutes of wrist rolls
- 1 minute of standing hip circles

Workout:

- 1 minute of wall plank with alternating shoulder taps
- 1 minute of wall-assisted mountain climbers
- 1 minute of wall-assisted dead bug extensions
- 1 minute of wall-assisted flutter kicks
- 1 minute of wall-assisted side plank leg lifts (30 seconds each side)

Cool down:

- 1 minute of deep breathing
- 2 minutes of wall-assisted standing forward fold
- 2 minutes of wall-assisted pigeon pose

Wellness practice: Drink at least 8 cups (64 ounces) of water daily to stay hydrated. Proper hydration is essential for optimal health and can improve digestion, cognitive function, and skin appearance.

Day 19: Upper Body Strength!

Build upper body strength for better posture and daily activities.

Warm-up:

- 2 minutes of gentle arm swings

- 2 minutes of shoulder circles

- 1 minute of gentle neck stretches

Workout:

- 1 minute of wall push-ups with alternating knee tucks

- 1 minute of wall-assisted inchworms

- 1 minute of wall-assisted plank up-downs

- 1 minute of wall-assisted T-plank rotations (30 seconds each side)

- 1 minute of wall-assisted reverse flyes

Cool down:

- 1 minute of deep breathing

- 2 minutes of wall-assisted chest stretch

- 2 minutes of wall-assisted tricep stretch

Wellness practice: Take a 15-minute walk outside during your lunch break or after dinner. Walking can help improve mood, digestion, and overall physical health.

Day 20: Lower Body Blast!

Challenge your lower body muscles for increased strength and endurance.

Warm-up:

- 2 minutes of gentle jogging in place
- 2 minutes of ankle circles
- 1 minute of hip circles

Workout:

- 1 minute of wall-assisted squat pulses
- 1 minute of wall-assisted step-ups (30 seconds each leg)
- 1 minute of wall-assisted single-leg glute bridges (30 seconds each leg)
- 1 minute of wall-assisted standing abduction (30 seconds each leg)
- 1 minute of wall-assisted standing adduction (30 seconds each leg)

Cool down:

- 1 minute of deep breathing
- 2 minutes of wall-assisted figure four stretch
- 2 minutes of wall-assisted standing quad stretch

Wellness practice: Drink a cup of herbal tea, such as chamomile or peppermint, before bedtime to promote relaxation and support digestion.

Day 21: Dynamic Stretching!

Incorporate dynamic stretching to improve flexibility, mobility, and range of motion.

Warm-up:

- 2 minutes of gentle high knees
- 2 minutes of arm circles

- 1 minute of standing side bends

Workout:

- 1 minute of wall-assisted leg swings (30 seconds each leg)

- 1 minute of wall-assisted standing chest opener

- 1 minute of wall-assisted seated hamstring stretch with toe reach

- 1 minute of wall-assisted dynamic lunge stretch (30 seconds each leg)

- 1 minute of wall-assisted standing hip flexor stretch (30 seconds each leg)

Cool down:

- 1 minute of deep breathing

- 2 minutes of wall-assisted butterfly stretch

- 2 minutes of wall-assisted seated forward fold

Wellness practice:

Perform 5 minutes of deep breathing exercises daily, focusing on inhaling and exhaling slowly and deeply. Deep breathing can help reduce stress, lower blood pressure, and increase lung capacity.

Day 22: Balance Booster!

Enhance your balance and coordination with challenging exercises.

Warm-up:

- 2 minutes of gentle marching in place

- 2 minutes of shoulder rolls

- 1 minute of knee lifts

Workout:

- 1 minute of wall-assisted tree pose (30 seconds each leg)

- 1 minute of wall-assisted single-leg calf raises (30 seconds each leg)

- 1 minute of wall-assisted single-leg squat hold (30 seconds each leg)

- 1 minute of wall-assisted warrior III (30 seconds each leg)

- 1 minute of wall-assisted single-leg hip hinges (30 seconds each leg)

Cool down:

- 1 minute of deep breathing

- 2 minutes of wall-assisted standing forward fold

- 2 minutes of wall-assisted quad stretch (1 minute each leg)

Wellness practice: Incorporate a 10-minute stretching routine after your workout to improve flexibility and aid muscle recovery. Stretching can also help to reduce post-workout soreness and increase overall range of motion.

Day 23: Full Body Challenge!

Combine upper, lower, and core exercises for a well-rounded workout.

Warm-up:

- 2 minutes of gentle jumping jacks

- 2 minutes of arm swings

- 1 minute of gentle spinal twists

Workout:

- 1 minute of wall-assisted squat to overhead reach

- 1 minute of wall push-ups with alternating leg lifts

- 1 minute of wall-assisted side plank with leg lift (30 seconds each side)

- 1 minute of wall-assisted reverse lunge with twist (30 seconds each leg)

- 1 minute of wall-assisted plank with alternating knee tucks

Cool down:

- 1 minute of deep breathing

- 2 minutes of wall-assisted chest stretch

- 2 minutes of wall-assisted hamstring stretch

Wellness practice: Try a 10-minute relaxation technique, such as progressive muscle relaxation or body scan meditation, to release muscle tension and promote overall relaxation.

Day 24: Core Challenge!

Strengthen your core muscles for improved balance, posture, and daily function.

Warm-up:

- 2 minutes of gentle side steps

- 2 minutes of torso twists

- 1 minute of gentle hip circles

Workout:

- 1 minute of wall-assisted straight-leg raises

- 1 minute of wall-assisted bicycle crunches

- 1 minute of wall-assisted plank with hip dips

- 1 minute of wall-assisted side plank with rotation (30 seconds each side)

- 1 minute of wall-assisted Russian twists

Cool down:

- 1 minute of deep breathing

- 2 minutes of wall-assisted seated forward fold

- 2 minutes of wall-assisted seated twist (1 minute each side)

Wellness practice: Incorporate 10 minutes of mindful walking into your daily routine. Focus on your breath, the sensations in your body, and the environment around you. Mindful walking can help reduce stress and increase overall mindfulness.

Day 25: Upper Body Strength Builder!

Increase upper body strength for better posture and ease in daily activities.

Warm-up:

- 2 minutes of gentle arm swings

- 2 minutes of shoulder rolls

- 1 minute of gentle neck stretches

Workout:

- 1 minute of wall-assisted decline push-ups

- 1 minute of wall-assisted plank to dolphin pose

- 1 minute of wall-assisted scapular push-ups

- 1 minute of wall-assisted standing tricep extensions

- 1 minute of wall-assisted YTWL exercises

Cool down:

- 1 minute of deep breathing

- 2 minutes of wall-assisted chest stretch

- 2 minutes of wall-assisted tricep stretch

Wellness practice: Include more vegetables and fruits in your meals to increase your intake of essential vitamins, minerals, and antioxidants. Aim for at least five servings of vegetables and fruits per day.

Day 26: Lower Body Endurance!

Build endurance and strength in your lower body muscles.

Warm-up:

- 2 minutes of gentle jogging in place

- 2 minutes of ankle circles

- 1 minute of hip circles

Workout:

- 1 minute of wall-assisted squat jumps

- 1 minute of wall-assisted lateral lunges with a pulse (30 seconds each leg)

- 1 minute of wall-assisted glute bridge with a hold

- 1 minute of wall-assisted single-leg standing calf raises (30 seconds each leg)

- 1 minute of wall-assisted single-leg deadlifts (30 seconds each leg)

Cool down:

- 1 minute of deep breathing

- 2 minutes of wall-assisted figure four stretch

- 2 minutes of wall-assisted standing hamstring stretch

Wellness practice: Set a goal to take regular movement breaks throughout your day, aiming for at least 250 steps per hour. This can help prevent prolonged sitting, associated with various health risks.

Day 27: Full Body Flow!

Combine upper, lower, and core exercises for a comprehensive workout.

Warm-up:

- 2 minutes of gentle jumping jacks

- 2 minutes of arm circles

- 1 minute of gentle spinal twists

Workout:

- 1 minute of wall-assisted squat to overhead press

- 1 minute of wall-assisted push-up to side plank (alternating sides)

- 1 minute of wall-assisted single-leg squat (30 seconds each leg)

- 1 minute of wall-assisted plank with alternating toe taps

- 1 minute of wall-assisted standing knee-to-elbow crunches

Cool down:

- 1 minute of deep breathing

- 2 minutes of wall-assisted chest stretch

- 2 minutes of wall-assisted butterfly stretch

Wellness practice: Practice 10 minutes of deep breathing or meditation in a quiet space to help reduce stress, improve focus, and increase overall well-being.

Day 28: Celebration Circuit!

Celebrate your progress with a challenging full-body workout that incorporates various exercises from the previous days.

Warm-up:

- 2 minutes of gentle high knees

- 2 minutes of shoulder rolls

- 1 minute of gentle hip circles

Workout:

- 1 minute of wall-assisted mountain climbers

- 1 minute of wall-assisted squat pulses

- 1 minute of wall-assisted plank with alternating shoulder taps

- 1 minute of wall-assisted side plank leg lifts (30 seconds each side)

- 1 minute of wall-assisted reverse lunge with twist (30 seconds each leg)

Cool down:

- 1 minute of deep breathing

- 2 minutes of wall-assisted standing forward fold

- 2 minutes of wall-assisted quad stretch (1 minute each leg)

Wellness practice: Reflect on your progress throughout the 28-day challenge and set new goals for your fitness journey. Consider incorporating more advanced Pilates exercises, exploring new wellness practices, or trying other forms of exercise to keep yourself engaged and motivated.

TESTIMONIALS

Introducing the inspiring stories of real people who have experienced the transformative power of the Wall Pilates Challenge! These incredible testimonials remind me daily why I'm so passionate about sharing the benefits of wall Pilates with others. The positive impact that this challenge has had on their lives – from improved flexibility and balance to increased energy levels and overall well-being – is truly remarkable. Each of these stories is a testament to the program's effectiveness and fuels my motivation to continue spreading the joy of wall Pilates. Read on and let their experiences inspire you to live a healthier, happier, and more fulfilling life.

"As a stay-at-home mom of three young kids, I constantly felt exhausted and overwhelmed. I needed something to help me regain my energy and get back in shape. That's when I discovered the Wall Pilates Challenge. I was hesitant at first, but the fact that it only required 10 minutes a day made it seem manageable. I noticed my flexibility, balance, and overall well-being improvements within the first week. Now, I can play with my kids without feeling tired, and I've even started to enjoy cooking healthy meals for my family. This challenge has truly been a lifesaver, and I'm so grateful for the positive changes it has brought to my life!" – **Emily, 34, Stay-at-home Mom**

"After retiring from a long career as a nurse, I wanted to focus on my health and well-being. I came across the Wall Pilates Challenge and decided to try it. The progressive nature of the workouts and the daily wellness practices have had a profound impact on my life. I've rediscovered my love for gardening and can now spend hours tending to my plants without discomfort. My friends have even commented on how much more vibrant and energetic I seem. I couldn't be happier with the results and would recommend the challenge to anyone looking to improve their quality of life." – **Susan, 68, Retiree**

"Working long hours at my desk job, I often experienced back pain and poor posture. I knew I needed to change, but finding the motivation and time to exercise was difficult. The

Wall Pilates Challenge seemed like the perfect solution. Each morning before work, I would dedicate 10 minutes to the workout, and the results were astounding. My posture has improved significantly, and I no longer suffer from back pain. I even started taking short walks during my lunch breaks, and my colleagues have noticed my increased energy and enthusiasm at the office. This challenge has been a life-changing experience for me." – **David, 51, Office Worker**

"As an entrepreneur, my days were filled with endless meetings, tight deadlines, and high stress levels. My health was suffering, and I knew I needed to find a way to incorporate exercise into my busy schedule. The Wall Pilates Challenge offered the perfect solution, with 10 minutes a day of effective, low-impact workouts. Within weeks, I noticed improved flexibility, strength, and balance, making everyday tasks much easier. I've even started hosting weekly Wall Pilates sessions at my office to share the benefits with my team. This challenge has truly transformed both my personal and professional life." – **Laura, 42, Entrepreneur**

"As a personal trainer, I've always been passionate about fitness, but my busy schedule left me little time to focus on my well-being. When I discovered the Wall Pilates Challenge, I was intrigued by the promise of noticeable results in just 10 minutes a day. I decided to try it and was amazed by its impact on my life. The daily workouts and wellness practices have improved my flexibility, balance, and strength and enhanced my ability to connect with clients on a deeper level. I can now empathize with their struggles and offer effective solutions, thanks to my personal experience with this challenge. It has been an invaluable addition to my life and career." – **Mike, 35, Personal Trainer**

CONCLUSION

In conclusion, the Wall Pilates Workout Book and the 28-Day Challenge have provided you with a diverse and comprehensive program to elevate your well-being through the power of wall Pilates. As you've progressed through the challenge and explored the variety of workouts, you've undoubtedly experienced remarkable improvements in flexibility, strength, balance, and overall health. We hope this journey has enriched your understanding of wall Pilates and inspired you to continue incorporating these beneficial exercises into your daily life. Consistency is the key to maintaining long-lasting results, so remember to revisit the workouts and wellness practices outlined in this book whenever you need a revitalizing boost.

As you move forward, let the inspiring testimonials from those who have experienced the transformative power of wall Pilates remind you of the incredible impact this practice can have on your life. Stay committed, challenge yourself, and embrace the positive changes that wall Pilates brings. Thank you for embarking on this journey with us, and we wish you continued success and happiness in your pursuit of a healthier, more vibrant life!

Made in the USA
Las Vegas, NV
20 May 2023